Road to Power

Since 1996, Bloomberg Press has published books for financial professionals, as well as books of general interest in investing, economics, current affairs, and policy affecting investors and business people. Titles are written by well-known practitioners, BLOOMBERG NEWS® reporters and columnists, and other leading authorities and journalists. Bloomberg Press books have been translated into more than 20 languages.

For a list of available titles, please visit our Web site at www.wiley.com/go/bloombergpress.

Road to Power

How GM's Mary Barra
Shattered the Glass Ceiling

Laura Colby

WILEY | **Bloomberg**
PRESS

Published by John Wiley & Sons, Inc., Hoboken, New Jersey.
Published simultaneously in Canada.

For general information on our other products and services or for technical support, please contact our Customer Care Department within the United States at (800) 762-2974, outside the United States at (317) 572-3993 or fax (317) 572-4002.

Wiley publishes in a variety of print and electronic formats and by print-on-demand. Some material included with standard print versions of this book may not be included in e-books or in print-on-demand. If this book refers to media such as a CD or DVD that is not included in the version you purchased, you may download this material at http://booksupport.wiley.com. For more information about Wiley products, visit www.wiley.com.

Library of Congress Cataloging-in-Publication Data:

Colby, Laura.
  Road to power : how GM's Mary Barra shattered the glass ceiling / Laura Colby.
    pages cm
  Includes bibliographical references and index.
  ISBN 978-1-118-97263-2 (cloth); ISBN 978-1-118-97266-3 (ebk); ISBN 978-1-118-97265-6 (ebk)
1. Barra, Mary. 2. General Motors Corporation. 3. Automobile industry and trade–United States–Biography. 4. Women executives–Biography. 5. Businesswomen–Biography. I. Title.
  HD9710.U52B333 2015
  338.7'629222092–dc23
  [B]
                                                                                    2014047584

Printed in the United States of America

10 9 8 7 6 5 4 3 2 1

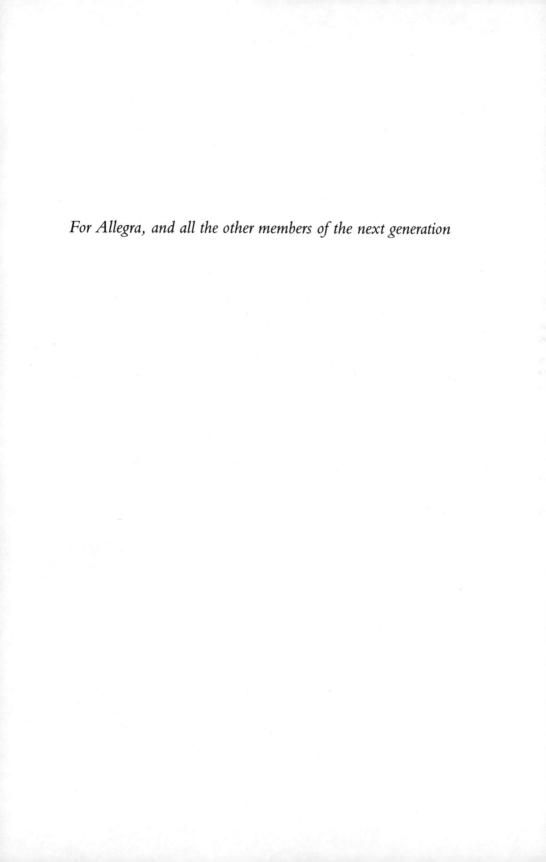

For Allegra, and all the other members of the next generation

Contents

Preface

"Just don't go there."

That was Mary Barra's advice when, in March 2012, she was asked at a meeting of Michigan's women in business organization, Inforum,[1] about whether she had experienced discrimination as a female manager during her career. Hard as that is to believe—coming from a rare woman engineer, who started on a factory floor at the age of 18 back in the early 1980s—Barra denied ever being held back by being female. "I never said, 'that happened to me because I'm a woman.'"

Like many women of her generation, Barra played down gender as her career advanced. And she rose through the ranks of General Motors, a company that caught on early to the idea that women make up not only a large portion of the potential workforce, but also a huge share of potential customers. Encouraging women to become leaders made business sense, executives told me over and over again, because women represent a large proportion of car buyers. GM's moves to include women didn't come in a vacuum, though: They followed a string of U.S. government actions that made the company take notice—including a discrimination lawsuit.

Pushed or not, GM has been more successful than most large companies at cultivating high-ranking women, especially starting with Barra's generation. Though the numbers of women on the board and in management still lag behind men, they are at least twice the average of other large publicly traded companies that make up the Standard & Poor's 500 index. Some 26 percent, or six of the 23 top corporate officers are women, and there's a cadre of female vice presidents behind them. That compares with 8 percent for the S&P 500 index companies.[2] There are four women on the company's 12-member board of directors, or 33 percent, versus an average of 18 percent for other S&P 500 companies.

GM, especially in 2014 after it was disclosed to have failed to recall millions of cars that had a potentially deadly defect for more than a decade, has been criticized time and again for its bureaucratic culture, where a focus on process can supersede common sense. Yet in reporting this book, one thing that has struck me is that the same obsession with systems and processes has had a big role in creating a cadre of women, including Barra, who are just now getting to the top.

GM executives began reaching out to women as early as the 1970s, as the women's liberation movement was changing the way workforces operated. The steps accelerated and became more concrete following the company's 1983 settlement of a decade-old employment discrimination complaint with the Equal Employment Opportunity Commission (EEOC). Under the landmark deal, reached while Mary Barra was a college student at what was then the General Motors Institute, GM agreed to set goals for the promotion of women and minorities and to report back to the EEOC on its progress. Managers were asked regularly where the women in their areas were, and were encouraged to seek out female talent.

Throughout her career, Barra had mentors both male and female who tried to make sure she got opportunities to grow and advance. Once she was designated a high-potential employee, she was rotated through different positions in the company, at times well beyond her comfort and skill level. By embracing those new challenges, Barra deepened her knowledge and skills and was able to become a better manager. She in turn helped other women, both informally and formally, including setting up an internal networking group for women at the company in the 1990s.

Barra went through a decades-long grooming process before ascending to the top. One of the most striking things about her career is how close she was to some of the most important inflection points in the company's history. Like an automotive Forrest Gump—but smarter—she was often just below the radar, not yet powerful enough to get noticed by outsiders. Still, she was there, soaking up knowledge, learning lessons from the company's successes and failures, and building a network of mentors and supporters.

Her first job out of college in the 1980s was at a factory that was one of the first North American plants to adopt Japanese manufacturing and management methods—which Barra would be instrumental in applying across the company years later. The experiment failed after its cars had safety issues, in a foreshadowing of a safety crisis Barra would face decades later as the company's chief. In the 1990s, when CEO John Francis "Jack" Smith Jr. tried to bring order and logic to GM's sprawling and bureaucratic culture, Barra was in the executive suite, working as his personal assistant. When the company was sliding toward bankruptcy, Barra was one of the top managers scrambling to invent a recovery plan. Following the government bailout, it was Barra who fought to keep executives' pay from being sliced and who helped build the new management team. As the company revamped its car models postbankruptcy, she was in charge of the effort. It was only after decades of steadily climbing the ranks and proving herself time and again that she finally won a job in the public eye.

Loath as she is to play the gender card, Barra had little choice but to "go there" once she was named chief executive officer of General Motors in December 2013. Hers is the highest position ever held by a woman at a global automaker and, given GM's size and importance to the country's economy, perhaps the most important corporate position ever held by a woman in the United States. Much was made of her gender in the news reports of her appointment. Media outlets, including *Bloomberg News* and *Bloomberg Businessweek*, which put her on its cover, wrote profiles. When attending the Detroit Auto Show in January 2014, just as she was taking on her new role, she was mobbed like a rock star.

Amid all the celebration, there was an undertone of condescension toward this woman with an electrical engineering degree, an MBA from Stanford, and more than 30 years of increasingly responsible positions at GM. Even the man who promoted Barra, her predecessor Dan Akerson, said that seeing her take the CEO role was "almost like watching your daughter graduate from college." Barra's pay was found to be less than Akerson's, until deferred compensation and stock were taken into account.

Little did she know then that within weeks that aura would be tarnished and she would face the greatest challenge of her career. The company had delayed for more than a decade recalling cars for a safety defect that has cost at least 45 customers their lives, a tragedy whose full scope is still being determined. GM—and Barra—were vilified in the Congress that had approved bailing out the bankrupt company only a few years earlier. There, too, gender became an issue. Some pundits even posited that Barra had been given the CEO role by Akerson only *because* she was female. They argued that she would present the company with a softer image and one that critics were less likely to attack.

Anyone who watched her interrogation in front of the House of Representatives and Senate panels investigating the ignition switch recall—where, ironically, many of the most hostile questioners were women—would reject the argument that she got a pass because she is female. "I am very disappointed, really, as a woman to woman," scolded Senator Barbara Boxer when Barra was unable to answer detailed questions about the recall during the first round of appearances in April.

There was also some friendly fire. In a national televised interview on NBC's *Today* show, Matt Lauer asked Barra whether she thought she could be both a "good mom" and CEO of the largest U.S. automaker,[3] a line of questioning that immediately drew criticism for its perceived sexism.[4] While Lauer responded that he would ask a male CEO a similar question, he gave no examples of having done so.

Of those who know Barra, who have followed her career, and who are familiar with the challenges facing the auto industry, rare is the person who argues that she is unqualified to lead GM. Most would say she got the job despite being a woman, rather than because of it. She has proved herself over decades, starting when she joined Pontiac as an 18-year-old cooperative education student. Along the way, she expanded her skills, made some smart decisions, formed key alliances, proved her intelligence, and did a lot of hard work.

In reporting this book, I learned that Barra, while exceptional, is not an outlier.

She is one of a cadre of women rising through the famously bureaucratic corridors of power at GM and who are just coming into their own. Many of them are engineers who were fearless about following their interests into areas where women were far fewer than they are today, while others are working in finance, marketing, and general management areas. Still, even with corporate programs that seek them out and aim to advance them, women remain underrepresented across the auto industry, including at GM.

This book aims to illuminate the steps Barra took in her career and, in so doing, to provide ideas for others to follow, whether they are aspiring engineers or accountants, parents of girls, teachers, or human resources executives at companies that want to stop shortchanging half of the population—and half their potential customers.

Barra attributes her own career to a love of math and science and a willingness to follow that interest. While women earn more than half of bachelor's and master's degrees in the United States today, they represent a far lower share of those earning degrees in so-called STEM fields (science, technology, engineering, and mathematics). The numbers drop even further after college: Though women earn about 20 percent of degrees in engineering, they represent only about 11 percent of those employed as engineers, and many drop out after a few years.[5] So recruitment, training, and support throughout a woman's career are just as important as education.

This book is being written less than a year into Barra's tenure in the top job, so the jury is still out as to whether she will be able to effect a lasting change in the way the 100-year-old company does business. Others have tried before, and failed. Barra aims to make GM nimble enough to compete in a challenging global market where the technology is changing drastically, and, as she put it, stop making "crappy cars." Her competitors aren't standing still, though. Her biggest task is to get beyond the taint of scandal surrounding GM's failure to recall the faulty ignition switch that has branded her tenure. Even as she tried to turn the page at the end of her first year, the company continued to unearth new defects that resulted in recalls.

Time may be on her side. At age 53 (she was born in December 1961), Barra could have a decade or more ahead of her as CEO. And just maybe, by the time she hands the baton over to a successor, we will be so used to seeing women in powerful corporate roles that she will be judged not on her gender, but on the results she obtains. And because Barra and a generation of women like her have dared to enter what was a man's world and pave the way for future generations, her successor could even be another woman. Maybe then we finally wouldn't have to "go there" anymore.

Notes

1. http://vimeo.com/38590869.
2. Jeff Green, "Women Left Off CEO Track Even After Securing High-Ranking Jobs," *Bloomberg News*, August 21, 2014.
3. www.today.com/video/today/55512578.
4. www.bloomberg.com/video/why-do-professional-women-get-the-mom-que stion-Mf~LSanIThiT7cjJ6pPEtg.html.
5. Nadya A. Fouad, Romila Singh, Mary E. Fitzpatrick, and Jane P. Liu, "Stemming the Tide: Why Women Leave Engineering," University of Wisconsin–Milwaukee, 2012.

Acknowledgments

T his book would not have been possible without the help of my Bloomberg News colleagues. First and foremost I'd like to thank Matt Winkler, for his backing of the idea and our coverage of women in business generally. A big thank you to Lisa Kassenaar, who heads Bloomberg's global women's project and who first suggested writing about Mary Barra. Lisa was a tireless advocate for the book from the beginning. I'm grateful to Reto Gregori and Jonathan Kaufman for allowing me to take the time to complete it. I'd especially like to thank John Lippert for sharing his vast knowledge of the auto industry and the people who run it, and for his insightful comments on the manuscript.

Other colleagues provided much-appreciated advice and encouragement, including Jason Kelly, Yalman Onaran, Phil Revzin, Angela Greiling Keane, Caroline Chen and Alan Crawford. I'd also like to thank my colleagues in Bloomberg's Detroit bureau, especially Jeff Green, Jamie Butters and Tim Higgins, whose superb work covering Barra and the ignition switch scandal I drew on. A shoutout also to Patrick Hayes and David White of Kettering University, Paige Plant of Detroit's National Automotive History Collection and Janet Driscoll at the Stanford graduate school of business library for their valuable guidance.

I'd also like to express my appreciation for all the current and former colleagues, teachers and classmates of Mary Barra—too numerous to name here—who were generous with their time and insight. I especially want to thank Tony Cervone, for understanding what the project was about, and Juli Huston-Rough, for helping to make things happen. And thank you to Mary Barra, for agreeing to speak with me.

Especially warm thanks to Naftali Raz for his unwavering support, logistical and otherwise.

Introduction

Dodge's La Femme: Women and Cars

Early one sunny August morning in 1888, a 39-year-old woman slipped out of her home in Mannheim, Germany, while her husband was still sleeping. She left a note for him, and with her sons, aged 13 and 15, climbed into the family car.

Bertha Benz drove south via Heidelberg and through the Black Forest to Pforzheim, a town in southwestern Germany, to visit her mother.[1] During the trip, Bertha's car, called a Motorwagen, had a couple of problems. One was a clogged fuel line, which she fixed with a hat pin. The other was trouble with an ignition switch. She used one of her garters to solve that one.

Bertha's journey, some 194 kilometers to her mother's house and back, was the first road trip ever, and it was taken by a woman. She just happened to be the wife of Karl Benz, the engineer who patented the first internal-combustion-powered automobile. It was thanks to Bertha's financial backing that she and Karl were able found the company that later became Mercedes-Benz.

So much of the mythology surrounding cars in our era has been perpetuated by male-dominated automakers and aimed at male drivers. That's why it became a global event when Mary Barra was named chief executive officer of General Motors in December 2013. It's less known that women have played an important role in the industry's development since its earliest days—and not just as the slinky hood ornaments so often seen in car advertising. The auto's promise of individual freedom, the ability to explore new territory, and the sheer thrill of driving have always appealed to women as well as men.

In the United States in the early twentieth century, Alice Ramsey made history by becoming the first woman to drive across the country, a trip that took more than a month on mostly unpaved roads. Ramsey, a 22-year-old housewife and Vassar graduate from Hackensack, New Jersey, was accompanied by three other women, none of whom knew how to drive. The women crossed paths with a manhunt for a killer in Nebraska and a Native American hunting party in Nevada that surrounded their vehicle with bows and arrows drawn.[2]

Ramsey's journey was reprised five years later by suffragettes,[3] who wanted to draw attention to the cause of votes for women. Alice Snitzer Burke and Nell Richardson drove a Saxon Roadster more than 10,000 miles from New York to California and back, stopping in dozens of towns along the way to rally support for the cause. (Congress didn't ratify the 19th amendment until six years later, in 1920.)

By that time, women had begun driving in significant numbers. Women had even earned patents for inventions that would become standard in future cars, including windshield wipers and turn signals.

As more women began to drive, some automakers began targeting them as a distinct market, offering smaller and cheaper models. In the 1920s, Chevrolet began selling the Utility Coupe, a low-priced closed sedan with storage trunk, as "the car for the Woman on the Farm."[4]

Perhaps the most famous car aimed directly at female drivers was launched in 1955, when Dodge's Plymouth marque produced a special edition of its Royal sedan dubbed La Femme. The car was a proto-Barbie confection with a pink and white exterior. The (male) designers came up with every feature they could think of that would appeal to women, from rosebud-printed seat covers to a rain cape, hat, and umbrella that matched the upholstery. The car also came with a pink shoulder bag containing driving "essentials" such as a makeup compact, comb, and lipstick holder. "By appointment to Her Majesty ... the American Woman," an advertisement proclaimed.[5]

Not too surprisingly, La Femme bombed, selling fewer than 1,000 units. It was scrapped the following year.

Since then, only a handful of cars have been aimed solely at women, though some have been marketed heavily to them. Barra's first job out of college in the 1980s was working at a Pontiac plant that made a car called the Fiero, whose advertising featured sexy, independent women at the wheel, at times literally leaving men in their dust. More recently, Ford Motor Company's Volvo division introduced a concept car at the 2004 Geneva Auto Show that was designed by and for women. The YCC, short for Your Concept Car, had features such as hybrid engine, the ability to alert the dealer when the car needed maintenance, and a headrest with a strategically placed slit to make room for a driver's ponytail.[6] The car was never put into production.

In 2007, General Motors executive Mary Sipes organized a training exercise for sport-utility vehicle (SUV) designers where men were outfitted with high heels, gloves with fake nails attached, and plastic garbage bags around their waists to simulate what it's like to get into a car carrying groceries and operate it dressed as a woman. She calls the exercise a bit "silly" but says it opened their eyes to the need for making sure cars appeal to all customers (about a third of GM's buyers are women).

Increasingly, carmakers are paying more attention to female customers and, if not creating so-called women's models, at least starting to offer features that will be more attractive to them, such as greater customization, high-grade materials, and in-vehicle technology such as assisted parking that makes a car easier to maneuver. Porsche in 2014 introduced a crossover vehicle called the Macan, aimed largely at women.[7] Unlike most of the German luxury company's vehicles, the Macan has a starting price tag of under $50,000. Fiat makes its 500 highly customizable with dozens of color variations. BMW's Mini also is intended to appeal to women.

There are good business reasons for catering to the female market. Women themselves purchase or are involved in the purchase of around

85 percent of all vehicles. And women hold 51 percent of all U.S. driver's licenses, a trend toward increased female presence that is also occurring in Canada and the United Kingdom, according to research by Frost & Sullivan.[8] In the United States, Europe, and even much of the developing world, more women are earning higher education degrees than men are. That implies that they will continue to narrow the wage gap with men and increase their purchasing power. "Women are a larger and more valuable customer segment than men," says Olivia Walker, a senior consultant at Frost & Sullivan who led the research.

Automakers also gradually began wooing women customers through education programs at their dealerships, something that Lexus is doing today. Chrysler in the early 1970s had a program called WOW!—short for "Women on Wheels"—that taught women how cars work, how to change a flat, and engine troubleshooting. Still, the tone was condescending, and an information pamphlet about the program shows a young woman inspecting a car's underbody with the caption, "What's a nice lady like you doing in a dirty place like this?"

In the 1980s, Chevrolet printed booklets with advice aimed at first-time car buyers (all of whom were depicted in cartoons as befuddled-looking women), entitled "How to buy a car or truck without becoming a wreck."[9] In 1986, Chevrolet produced a pamphlet to enlighten its dealers about how to treat women as customers. Under the heading "Some women's figures you should be watching," the booklet pointed out that 44 percent of new vehicles were purchased by women and 87.5 percent of all new vehicle purchases involved a woman. Salesmen were advised that "women shouldn't be 'dear' to you, or 'honey' or 'sweetie.'"[10] "No woman wants to be ignored, or treated like the brainless 'little woman,'" Chevy advised its dealers.

Dealers ignored the advice at their peril. Dan Akerson, the General Motors CEO who preceded Barra, told reporters how in the early years of his marriage he had walked out of a Chevrolet dealership and bought a Japanese car instead because the salesman treated his wife so poorly. "The guy called her 'the little woman,'" he recalled. "She got so angry she was almost in tears and said, 'I'm not buying a car at this place.' It was the first Toyota I bought."[11]

Even today, car companies have been slow to change the way they market vehicles. In 2014—as the first woman took the wheel of a global auto maker—auto shows featured scantily clad women alongside the newest car models, though, unlike in earlier decades, they are well informed about the car's features.[12] Frost & Sullivan's report found that 50 percent of women customers were dissatisfied with their cars, and three out of four females felt misunderstood by car companies.

Barra's rise to the CEO post gives hope to many in the industry that some of these gaffes will finally get redressed. Feminist icon Gloria Steinem recalled how, when she started *Ms.* magazine in 1972, she had been rebuffed by auto companies when she tried to get them to buy advertisements. "They always said, 'No, only men buy cars. Men make the decisions,'" she told Bloomberg Television shortly after Barra took over. "So I have a special joy in seeing a woman as [CEO] of General Motors."[13]

Notes

1. www.bertha-benz.de/indexen.php?sub=2&col=b&inhalt=pers_erstefahrt.
2. Biography, Automotive Hall of Fame, www.automotivehalloffame.org/ind uctee/alice-huyler-ramsey/177/.
3. "Two Noted Suffragists Travel 10,000 Miles in Saxon Roadster," Advertisement, Vertical File on Women, National Automotive History Collection, Detroit Public Library.
4. Advertisement, Vertical File on Women, National Automotive History Collection, Detroit Public Library.
5. Ibid.
6. www.volvoclub.org.uk/press/pdf/presskits/YCCPressKit.pdf.
7. Kyle Stock, "Porsche for Her," *Bloomberg Businessweek*, August 11–24, 2014, 58.
8. www.frost.com/prod/servlet/press-release.pag?docid=291103428.
9. Ibid.
10. Vertical File on Women, National Automotive History Collection, Detroit Public Library.
11. Tim Higgins, "Akerson Led GM from IPO to End of 'Government Motors,'" *Bloomberg News*, December 11, 2013.
12. Angela Greiling Keane and Siddarth Philip, "Go-Go Boots Part of Pitch Even as Barra Breaks Ceiling," *Bloomberg News*, January 16, 2014.
13. www.bloomberg.com/video/steinem-special-joy-to-see-mary-barra-as-gm-c eo-UMXzGd5jS46~hEaE~SBBdw.html.

Chapter 1

The Firebird:
A Childhood Dream

Barbara Gesaman was having a devil of a time making her sculpture for art class at Crary Junior High in Waterford Township, Michigan. There were toothpicks and glue, and she couldn't get them to stick together, let alone stand up into a three-dimensional structure.

Then she looked across the room to discover whether her classmates were doing any better. She wanted to see in particular how one girl was doing, the one who always built the best projects and who was in the corps of assistants who helped the science teachers in their labs.

Sure enough, her structure was impressive. "It was some kind of Ferris wheel," says Gesaman, who remained a friend through high school. "She had a great sense of spatial relationships. I think she was already an engineer."

The girl was Mary Makela. The daughter of Ray Makela, a long-time worker at General Motors, and Eva Makela, née Pyykkonen, a bookkeeper, Mary excelled in school. "I liked math and science, and they encouraged me to pursue that," says Mary, now Mary Barra. Her parents, both of Finnish ancestry, had grown up in the Great Depression. "They learned a lot and both had a lot of life struggles by growing up in that time," she says.

Neither parent went to college. Eva Makela attended a two-year associates program to become a bookkeeper, while Ray followed the skilled-tradesman process to become a journeyman die maker. He worked for General Motors Corporation in nearby Pontiac, as did many of the breadwinners in Waterford at that time. Eva valued education and insisted that her children, Mary and older brother Paul, attend college no matter what.

A community of modest-sized but well-kept homes, Waterford Township is dotted with an archipelago of 34 small lakes. In the short Michigan summers, local children rode their bikes down the town's shady streets to the homes of friends who lived on Watkins Lake or Elizabeth Lake, where they swam, glided in small sailboats, or hung out on the sandy shores.

The bucolic life contrasted with political strife taking place in the 1960s and 1970s. The 1967 riots in Detroit had sent many white families fleeing to the suburbs, and a similar pattern took place in Pontiac, about 30 miles to the northwest. The city's population had surged as African Americans, many from the South, flocked there from the 1920s onward to seek work in the auto industry. Pontiac reached a peak population of 85,000 people in 1970 and housed several auto plants, including the Pontiac Motor factory where Ray Makela worked. So many white families settled in surburban Waterford Township, about seven miles from Pontiac, that it became known locally as "white Waterford."

In the early 1970s, Detroit, backed by regional courts, began trying to integrate its schools by busing. Local officials argued that the city's own school district had become so racially segregated that it needed to bus in white students from outlying suburban school districts in order to integrate the schools—a decision that upset many suburban parents who had fled the city. In 1971, a branch of the Ku Klux Klan dynamited 10 school buses in Pontiac rather than have them be used for integration.[1] The Detroit busing plan eventually was appealed to the U.S. Supreme

Court as *Milliken v. Bradley*. The court ruled against busing by a 5 to 4 margin in 1974, a crushing blow to integration efforts. A quarter century later, Waterford was still 93 percent white.[2]

In Waterford, a factory worker without a college degree could afford a home with a yard, perhaps a small boat, and of course a car. A strong economy at the time kept GM's Pontiac Motor plant humming, and overtime fattened paychecks.

"My whole life growing up, I can't remember my father ever not being at work," Barra says, unlike later years when furloughs of autoworkers were regular events as foreign competitors cut into market share. "He worked a lot of overtime. The company was crunching out new models and the dies were changing each time you did that."

Had he been born in a different time, Ray Makela would have become an engineer rather than a factory hand, Barra says. Instead, he worked for 39 years as a die maker and was a member of the United Auto Workers union. Making dies is one of the more complex tasks in manufacturing, requiring a high degree of skill. Dies are tools used for shaping components of manufactured products, mostly using a press. Like a mold, the die needs to be customized to the product it is making. Dies have to be extremely precise; at times they can deviate from specifications by no more than one-thousandth of one inch. The trade requires years of either on-the-job training or a combination of trade school and apprenticeship.

Makela was a natural tinkerer. He had a workshop in his basement where he made things in his spare time or fixed household appliances. "It was a time when everyone fixed their own car, and changed their own oil," Barra recalls. "He did all that." Barra's older brother Paul did most of the dirty work, while she helped her mother with household chores. When she was done, she was allowed to work beside her father, whom she remembers taking apart a curling iron of hers that had gone on the blink.

Sometimes he brought home new cars from the Pontiac factory, which she was allowed to explore. "That was a big part of my life growing up, being excited about new cars," she says. She recalls an older cousin who had a Pontiac Firebird convertible, red with a white top. "I remember seeing it and loving it when I was 10 or 11 years old," she says.

Every year, the local car dealers would paper over their windows in the fall, when the next year's new models were coming out. The whole family got to see the unveiling when the new models were shown.

While her father supported her interest in science and fueled her curiosity about cars, Barra credits her mother, Eva, with pushing her to academic excellence. "My mom became very passionate about education," she says. Eva Makela wanted the next generation of her family to have the educational opportunities she had missed in her own life—it didn't matter what you studied, just that you did study. Over and over, she said, "You're going to college," not just to her own two children, but to those of her seven siblings.

Mrs. Makela, who was also a skilled seamstress, didn't care what career path her children followed, as long as they graduated from college and worked hard at whatever they did. "Working hard was important," Barra says. "You worked before you played. It was instrumental."

Barra's brother, Paul Makela, also heeded his mother's advice. After earning both his undergraduate and medical degrees at Detroit's Wayne State University, Makela is now a gynecological surgeon in the Detroit suburbs, where he performs state-of-the-art operations using robotic tools and computers.

At Waterford Mott High School, Mary was smart, but not a nerd. She was friendly and well-liked. She wore her brown hair in the shoulder-length, Farrah Fawcett style cut of the times, with looping curls at the side. She had glasses with large, round frames, and a warm smile. Classmates who remember her say she had an ability to talk to everybody, whether they were boys in the auto shop class or the kids with the high IQs who took physics and calculus. Mary was a member of the latter group: Her graduating class in 1980 had 10 students who earned a perfect 4.0 grade point average, and she was one of them.

In the late 1970s, while the country was recovering from the end of the Vietnam era and Watergate, life in Waterford harked back to an earlier era. A typical after-school activity might be heading across the street from the high school to the corner of Pontiac Lake and Scott Lake Road for soft-serve ice cream at Custard Corner or to the Big Boy on Dixie Highway. On weekends, kids went to one of several local cinemas, roller-skating at the Rolladium, or bowling at the 300 Bowl. They also hung out at the Pontiac Mall, later called the Summit Place Mall.

Mary Barra stayed away from the house parties that were often held on weekends, where drinking and other typical teen transgressions took place, said one former classmate. She was close friends with a cheerleader, Lisa Christos, who was part of the squad that was ranked eighth in the nation. Christos defied the cheerleader stereotypes: Like Mary, she was a member of the National Honor Society, and was one of the 10 students with a 4.0 grade point average.

Mary followed her parents' lead and work ethic, earning extra money at Felice's Quality Market, a grocery store in nearby Pontiac. "It was a nice family place," she recalls, chuckling at its slogan, "Where 'quality' is our middle name."

The summer before senior year, she attended a camp where she learned the skills she'd need the following year as she took on her first managerial assignment: coeditor of the school yearbook, *Polaris*. She learned how to size and crop photos, balance the different elements in a page layout, and edit articles.

That's where classmates first got a hint of her potential future as a manager. The yearbook was a huge project: The editors had to manage the deadlines throughout the school year, and get staffers to comply with them. There were a lot of different personalities. Though Mary shared the job with her classmate Barbara Gesaman, there was little doubt who was in charge. "She took the lead," Gesaman says. The biggest challenge was the photographers, she remembers. You'd have to be sure that they would actually attend the games that they said they were going to see, sometimes more than one in an evening, and then select photos that were of publication quality.

Eric Stileski, one of the photo staff, recalls Mary being extremely organized and businesslike, portioning out the assignments and making the photographers aware that if they agreed to cover an event, they'd be expected to deliver.

"She'd say, 'Okay, so you are going to do this, right?'" Stileski recalls. Then when he brought back the pictures, there were meetings to go over the prints and decide which ones would be used. "I would point out which ones I liked, and why," he said. When there were disagreements, "she was the one who decided."

There was little drama, Stileski says, even if it felt strange to take orders from a classmate. Gesaman says Mary got the staff to pull together as a team—a skill that she would repeatedly be cited for throughout her later career. She'd say, "Okay, we've got to get this done by a certain deadline. Can you take care of this part, and can you do that?" She worked hard, and expected others to do the same.

Barra's sense of humor—not often apparent in her public appearances today, where she can be stiff and resort to business school jargon—shows throughout the yearbook, with jokey captions and photos of classmates. The winners of the school spirit award are shown swapping genders, with the boy wearing a cheerleader's skirt and the girl in football shoulder pads. Gesaman, voted most valuable to the class, is shown absconding with a box labeled "class funds." Mary didn't spare herself from the good-natured skewering. Voted the girl most likely to succeed, she posed with her male counterpart, Mark Adamcyzk, for the yearbook next to a cutout posterboard that made it look like both of them were wearing only barrels and suspenders and on their way to the poorhouse.

In Mary's senior year, she decided to attend Michigan State University and major in math, her favorite subject. She had even chosen a roommate. Only months before school was to start, a classmate told her about another option, a school called General Motors Institute (GMI), based in Flint. She was amazed to find that with GMI's cooperative program, she could study, get work experience, and pay for her schooling with the wages she earned. "I wasn't sure how I was going to pay for school," she says. "My parents had saved for the first year, but [GMI] seemed very attractive to me because I could pay my own way. Knowing my dad had just retired and my mom was working part-time, it seemed the responsible thing to do."

So, when she told classmate Kent Land that she was going to work in a Pontiac plant after high school, he could barely believe it. "I was shocked," says Land, a former yearbook staffer who is now married to Barbara Gesaman. "Working in a plant? I thought she'd be doing something more than that." Then Mary explained that she would be a line worker for only a short while, so that she could learn how cars were made. She was going to become an engineer, and ultimately, she'd be running the place.

Notes

1. Associated Press, "Six Michigan Klansmen Arrested in Pontiac School Bus Shootings," *Washington (PA) Observer-Reporter*, September 10, 1971, A5.
2. www.twp.waterford.mi.us/Departments/Development-Services/Community-Planning-and-Development/PDF/WaterfordTwpCensus2000Info.aspx.

Chapter 2

The Red Chevette: Driving Lessons

"Cluck-*cluck*. Cluck-*cluck*. Cluck-*cluck*."

Every day, as 17-year-old Diana Tremblay entered the cafeteria at the iron foundry where she worked in Defiance, Ohio, one of the workers accompanied her footsteps with squawking and clucking noises, imitating a chicken.

After this went on for a while, Tremblay, who had just started her first year at General Motors Institute, where she was training in industrial management, had had enough. She walked up to the man, a forklift driver in his 30s, and asked him, "What is it? Why do you keep clucking at me? Do you want to talk to me? My name's Diana."

The man turned bright red and was too embarrassed to reply. The clucking stopped. Later, Tremblay became his boss as she took on more responsibility in the plant, which melted, poured, and finished the iron used for car engines. "It was one of those little tests to see how you're going to handle it," she says.

At an assembly plant in Pontiac, Michigan, at about the same time, 18-year-old Mary Makela was getting a hands-on education about what life was like on the factory floor. It was noisy and dirty and rough. And then there were the catcalls.

"They weren't used to seeing a lot of women in the plant," Barra says. "Every time I turned this one corner in the Pontiac plant, this guy would kind of yell," she says. "Finally, I walked over and asked him, 'Why do you do that?' He said, 'I don't know,'" she says, laughing. "Well, can't we just say hi?" she asked. "It was a very different environment than it is now. It was a good introduction into the world of work, compared with working at Dairy Queen."

There was also tension between management and workers, who had to do their line jobs at speeds set by management trying to meet production and cost goals. Instead of the booming output of the 1960s and early 1970s that created the need for overtime, General Motors had recently been forced to lay off workers. Barra's father had been a member of the United Auto Workers (UAW), "so I understood the union representation, but frankly I didn't *comprehend* it," Barra says. "It was an eye-opening experience."

In the fall of 1980, the U.S. auto industry was reeling after a decade that had upended many of the assumptions on which it had been built. One was the belief that the gasoline for powerful American cars would remain cheap. In 1973, oil-producing Arab nations had imposed an embargo on exports to the United States because of its support for Israel in the Arab-Israeli war. The price of oil soared, and long lines at the pumps became a fixture of the evening news. In 1979, President Jimmy Carter brokered a peace between Egypt and Israel, but Iran's revolution deposed the Shah and cut off that country's supply of oil, creating another oil crisis. By the time Mary began working at Pontiac, the price of oil had surged almost sevenfold to $21.59 a barrel from $3.18 in 1970, according to U.S. Energy Information Administration data. Car sales, meanwhile, plummeted to 9.3 million units at an annualized pace in May 1980, and then even further to 8.8 million (annualized) in December 1981—a low not seen again until February 2009 following the financial crisis that helped tip GM into bankruptcy.[1]

Another shattered assumption was that Americans would continue to prefer American cars. Dennis Pawley, who had worked as a paint shop supervisor at GM's plant in Pontiac at the time, told *Bloomberg Markets* writer John Lippert how he and others had watched a GM film in the mid-1970s that predicted Japanese carmakers could capture 10 percent of the American market. "With the arrogant mentality we had, everyone sat there and laughed," Pawley said.[2]

By the fall of 1980, they weren't laughing anymore. Chrysler had needed a government bailout the previous year. Japanese carmakers, especially Honda, were increasing market share as consumers sought more fuel-efficient and reliable models instead of gas-guzzlers. The U.S. carmakers had been caught flat-footed by the Japanese advance, as Honda's Civic and other Japanese models offered fuel economy and a level of reliability in the small cars that Detroit couldn't match. American carmakers were scrambling to produce a range of more fuel-efficient models—but it could take years to bring out those new models. In the meantime, the companies had to retrofit catalytic converters onto existing cars to meet newly imposed government standards. (Today, the three largest Japanese carmakers—Toyota, Honda, and Nissan—account for a third of the U.S. market.[3])

It was during this time of change that Mary began her studies at General Motors Institute (GMI). Founded in 1919 as a vocational school and acquired by General Motors in 1926, GMI followed a cooperative education model, an unusual academic system for the United States. Each student was "sponsored" by a division of GM—in reality, students had applied to and been hired by the division that sponsored them. The student-employees were paid for time they spent working at a car plant and were given two 12-week breaks per year to study at the university. After five years, they earned a degree in either engineering or industrial administration, a management major.

"It was more of a job that gives you an education, rather than an education that gets you a job," says Paul Bascobert, who graduated in 1986. GMI was the automotive equivalent of the Air Force Academy or West Point—rigorous, specialized training combined with general academics and indoctrination into the company's culture.

Female students were relatively new for the school. Apart from a brief period during World War II when college-educated women were trained for specific factory roles to replace men who were serving overseas, women hadn't attended in numbers until the 1970s. By the early

1980s, when Diana Tremblay and Mary attended, women made up as much as 32 percent of each year's class. Many of the women were concentrated in the industrial administration major that was perceived as easier than engineering, which involved more technical courses. In Mary's year, more than half the 29 industrial administration students were female. In electrical engineering, her chosen major, there were only 17 women out of 64 students. The faculty was still overwhelmingly male, with fewer than 10 women out of 135 in total.

Kettering Graduates

Several of GM's highest-ranking women attended the former General Motors Institute, now known as Kettering University.
1. Mary Barra, BS, electrical engineering, 1985, Chief Executive Officer
2. Grace Lieblein, BS, industrial engineering, 1983, Vice President
3. Diana Tremblay, BS, industrial administration, 1982, Vice President
4. Alicia Boler-Davis participated in a high school program for aspiring engineers, 1986, Senior Vice President

---

Source: Kettering University.

"I picked electrical engineering because a lot in the electrical world is based on math, and because my drafting skills weren't very good," Barra says. "Everything now is done on computer, but back then you were drawing everything, and my drafting professor was not impressed with my line quality."

Each year's class was divided into two groups, A and B, that alternated periods on campus with time working in a factory or other GM location. Group A would be on campus taking classes while group B would be working in a plant. Members of the two groups took the same menu of classes in math and basic sciences, engineering skills, management, and humanities; they had the same professors and participated in the same clubs or Greek life. But they might never meet half of their classmates. Longtime GM engineer Grace Leiblein, today the company's vice president for global quality, graduated in 1983 but never met Barra because they were in different sections. In Mary's graduating class there were about 350 students, split between the two sections.

GMI's academic program was intense, with students needing 140 credits to graduate, versus 120 for most traditional universities. A freshman electrical engineering major might take classes in communication, programming, manufacturing, chemistry, and differential calculus in a single semester. Between lectures and laboratory time, students could spend 20 hours or more in class each week, and many hours more studying as professors jammed a full semester's work into 12 weeks. There was no spring break or long summer holiday; the work part of the program started in the summer right after graduation from high school.

Most students worked at GM locations close to their hometowns so they could live with their parents during their work rotations, but they moved every six to 12 weeks between campus and job.

Mary marshaled her savings from her after-school job at Felice's grocery store to put a down payment on her first car: a Pontiac Firebird similar to the one her cousin had owned and that had sparked her interest in cars years earlier. Then she thought twice, and decided that she couldn't afford the Firebird and still pay all her living expenses at school. So she settled on a Chevrolet Chevette, a small, practical car aimed at people on a budget—especially women. "It had no options, an AM radio, and crank windows, but it was a very reliable car," she says. The one concession to the dreamed-of Firebird: It was also red.

Flint is a city whose history has been closely tied to the auto industry. Native son William C. Durant, who had managed the Buick car company, founded an automaker of his own in Flint back in 1908, calling it General Motors. The town expanded along with the car industry, reaching a peak population of just under 200,000 in the 1960s. But by the early 1980s, Flint's population had already shrunk by about 20 percent. By the end of the decade, it had become a symbol of the decline in U.S. auto manufacturing and was featured in Michael Moore's 1989 documentary about 30,000 GM job losses, *Roger & Me*, whose portrayal of the city in denial of its problems is still a sore point locally.

The jobs were already disappearing in 1980, and with businesses shutting down, crime was on the rise. For GMI students, there was little to do in Flint. They could go for Mexican food at Chichi's, have ice cream at Howard Johnson's, or guzzle beer at the dimly lit bar across the street, which was frequented by factory rats from the town's auto plants. (The United States wouldn't raise the drinking age to 21 until 1984.)

On campus, there were a handful of intramural clubs, including motor sports and weight lifting. That left the sororities and fraternities as the main source of a social life. Mary joined Beta Theta Pi, the so-called little sister organization affiliated with the national fraternity of the same name that is one of the oldest in the country.

Pledging in those days was less harsh than the hazing that makes news headlines today. Would-be sisters had to memorize the Greek alphabet and see how many times they could recite it without error while holding a lit match. The girls staged pranks, such as "kidnapping" a pledge master and sending the rushes on a scavenger hunt to find him. Once, a friendly Flint police officer made a mock arrest of the pledge master, complete with finger printing and mug shot.

The 20 or 30 sorority sisters remained close throughout their school years, serving as informal mentors. Terri Lynch-Caris, a Beta Theta Pi sister who was three years behind Mary at GMI, sometimes got help with her calculus homework from the upperclass-woman. "She was really smart and charismatic, and people wanted to be around her," says Lynch-Caris, who went on to earn a PhD in engineering at the University of Michigan, and now teaches at GMI's successor school, Kettering University.

Since GMI had only enough dorm space for freshmen, students had to find their own housing for the on-campus periods. Sorority and fraternity housing was considered to be safer than a downtown apartment in Flint. Most of the Beta fraternity brothers lived in a house near a lake in Fenton, some 17 miles south of Flint. They hired a bus to shuttle them to campus and, outside of classes and socializing with the little sisters, spent little time on campus. Mary began dating one of them—a slightly older mechanical engineering student named Tony Barra.

Weekends were spent studying or at parties at the lake house in Fenton, across from the town's boat launch. Students sometimes went boating in fine weather, or drank beer and danced to disco music. Most of the free time was spent on homework. "We thought we were partiers," Lynch-Caris says, "but it was pretty tame."

Ironically, the little sister organization that Mary belonged to would fall victim to a 1988 decision by the fraternity that having female affiliates was too risky. In 1988, the national governing body of Beta Theta Pi decided to shut down all of its little sister organizations, citing insurance concerns and fears that the women would become privy to some of the fraternity's secret rituals.[4]

In class, Mary stood out for her leadership skills, said one of her former professors, Mo Torfeh. A professor of electrical engineering who still teaches at Kettering, Torfeh specializes in control systems. In every class, Torfeh says, there is a handful of students who want to get to know the professor and have him know them. Mary was one such student. "She was outstanding and smart. You could see the teamwork, the creativity, and the calculation," he says.

In Torfeh's two-hour lab, students are put into groups and assigned a problem to solve. They have to design control systems, perform simulations of the various systems, verify which actually work to solve the problem, and then pick one and build it.

Mary threw herself into this work, Torfeh says. As she had a couple of years earlier working on Waterford Mott's yearbook, she took charge of the group, divvying up the different responsibilities and assigning them to her classmates. She made sure the group completed its tasks in the allotted time, unlike other students, some of whom couldn't finish in the two hours. Some students cut corners, Torfeh says, but Mary was conscientious about getting everything done right. He said he saw those same skills at work during Barra's first months at GM, when she created a team of her own and began putting into place new systems that would catch defective car parts earlier.

There was a lot of pressure during the work periods as well. "It's really a long-term interview," says Lynch-Caris, the daughter of a millwright, who worked in an iron foundry while at GMI. "Over those five years, people are interviewing you and judging you 100 percent of the time.

"Initially, they look at you as if to say, 'What are *you* doing here?'" she recalls. There would be challenges, such as a boss assigning a seemingly impossible task, like testing out parts for a new production at the same time as a line was running. "You have to step up," she says.

GM had just gone through a series of layoffs, and under union rules the last hired was the first fired. That meant that the younger workers, and women who had been hired following efforts to increase the percentage of female staff, had been the first to go. So the GMI kids were working side by side with union men in their 40s, 50s, and 60s. The old-timers were constantly testing them. One student recalls being told to repair a machine that needed a spare part. The problem was that the machine and the part were no longer made. She recalls scouring the scrapyard behind the plant on advice from other workers and finally finding the part among the discarded machinery.

The atmosphere could be intimidating. Every girl who entered the plant ran a gauntlet of hoots and whistles—or clucks. One woman, who was assigned to the plant supervisor's office, remembers that workers from the factory floor and from a neighboring plant would stop by to gape at a teenager in a miniskirt. Another recalls how some of the men secretly rigged up an air hose under her desk, so that it blew her dress up when she sat down. Yet another tells of workers pinning her to a wall with a forklift and an older man, who'd helped train her and been a mentor, putting the moves on her the one time they found themselves alone together. "You'd never tell anyone," she says.

There were no female authority figures to turn to for help. Karen Palmer, whose first assignment was riveting nuts into 18-wheelers at GM Truck in Pontiac, Michigan, says there was only one electrical engineer who was female out of 20 at the plant. There were no female managers. Palmer toughed out a stint as "Rosie the Riveter" and just waved when she got catcalls. She went on to get her PhD at the Massachusetts Institute of Technology, where she says her training at GMI gave her the confidence and academic chops to succeed. Today, she teaches at Kettering.

Male students were also tested. "It was a rough environment, coming right out of high school," says Paul Bascobert, who worked in a plant in upstate New York. "There were people on the floor who gave everyone a difficult time. They could be particularly tough on women."

Not Just Cars

Kettering numbers many top executives among its alumni, not all of them in the auto industry.
1. Samuel Maurice Cossart Walsh, Chief Executive, Rio Tinto PLC (mining)
2. Rodney O'Neal, President and CEO, Delphi Automotive (auto parts)
3. E. Stanley O'Neal, former Chairman/CEO, Merrill Lynch & Co. (brokerage)
4. Troy Clarke, President/CEO, Navistar International (farm equipment)
5. David Kenny, Chairman/CEO, The Weather Channel (media)
6. Robert Kagle, general partner, Benchmark Capital (venture capital)
7. Kent Nelson, former chairman/CEO, United Parcel Service (shipping)

Source: Bloomberg.

The second year, when many students might wind up supervising line workers more than twice their age, could be even tougher. "Here you are, a college student, and you're supervising 60 workers on the line," says Jackie Kelm, Bascobert's sister, who graduated in 1986 with a BS in mechanical engineering. "It was rough. It was scary. They screamed and yelled. The work was tough, and you had to be tough to do it."

The testing might extend to disappearing when the student's back was turned, or showing up late. The student managers did have some leverage over the workers: They could write them up, or dock pay for serious insubordination. There were other ways of showing who was in charge, too. A worker who was disruptive or uncooperative could get the janitorial shift, or be assigned to a different machine than his usual one. That meant he would have to spend his shift adjusting to the new equipment rather than reading a book or hanging out with the guys. In extreme cases, a student supervisor could "lose" a troublemaker's paycheck when handing them out on a Friday afternoon, forcing the worker to forgo his Friday night trip to the bar with coworkers and wait until Monday for a duplicate to be issued.

But punitive measures were used only sparingly. Graduates said they worked hard to build a bond with workers, which was more effective than punishment. Some women did quit, but most toughed it out. The relationships they built in the plant paid dividends when students needed a sympathetic foreman or advice from an experienced line manager.

Women who tended to emphasize teamwork were especially adept at building those relationships. "It was a really fabulous experience," says Jackie Kelm, who now works as a leadership consultant. "Over time you build respect."

Barra agrees. "I don't regret it. I think it was a great opportunity to understand the core of the business," she says. The hazing she got was mild. It helped that she worked together with her roommate, Cathy Herritt, as a quality inspector at the Pontiac plant. "We got to know the people around us, and they taught us the business," she says.

Empathizing with workers came naturally for a large proportion of the students, who, like Barra, were the second or even the third generation in their families to go into the auto industry. Many were the first in their families to attend college, and had grown up listening to dinner table conversation about life in the plant. Sometimes there were even tensions at home, though, says Lynch-Caris, the GMI professor. "My father was in the UAW, and I was going to be a salaried manager," says Lynch-Caris, whose own son is now attending Kettering. Living out that conflict in her family helped her be more sensitive to workers at the plant. "The experience during your formative years teaches you not only how to work in that world, but also how to build relationships and to treat people with respect," says Bascobert, who now is the president of an online marketing start-up.

Those skills and the toughness they developed on the factory floor put GMI graduates miles ahead of their peers who were studying only in the classroom at more traditional colleges. For Barra, the schooling provided deep understanding of what went on at the most basic levels of the company, the nitty-gritty of how cars are made, and the people who make them.

And she became hooked on manufacturing. After finishing her sophomore year rotations, she applied to work for the rest of her schooling at a Pontiac plant that was just coming on line. It was an experimental plant that would use Japanese-inspired manufacturing methods to produce a sporty new small car. It was called the Fiero.

Notes

1. U.S. Auto Sales annualized total: Bloomberg data.
2. John Lippert, "The Fall of Detroit," *Bloomberg Markets*, November 2007, 106.
3. Japanese car market share source: BB Industries.
4. www.betathetapi.org/documents/policies_code/position_little_sisters.pdf.

Chapter 3

The Fiero: Trial by Fire

The pouty young woman with the Farrah Fawcett hairdo puts on black aviator glasses, then leaps like a ninja to a half-crouch beside the door of her red car. She's wearing white jeans, red boots, and a red jacket. High-pitched guitars play. The commercial cuts to a scene of the woman driving down an empty road, interspersed with spots of her vamping for the camera like a model in a cosmetics or shampoo commercial. "Fuel-injected and economical," the male narrator intones. "Pontiac builds *excitement.*"

The Pontiac Fiero was one of General Motors' most successful launches of the 1980s. A sporty little car, the Fiero was a two-seater with a low-slung profile that evoked pricier and faster vehicles such as Chevrolet's Corvette. It had a tapered front hood with retractable headlights that popped up like the eyes of an insect, a jaunty racer back, and a shortened tail.

The Fiero's body was made out of plastic, rather than the heavier metal used for most cars at the time; it was hailed as an engineering feat—and promised that its body would never rust. Its engine was a low-powered V-4 located in the middle of the body, rather than under the hood or trunk. Billed as a "commuter car," the Fiero got great mileage for its era, and the car had a starting price tag of just under $8,000 when it was introduced, making it attractive to young drivers—especially working women—on limited budgets.

At the same time, the car looked like the muscle cars of the previous decade and was marketed more for its sexy, sports car–like silhouette than its practical, commuter-friendly aspects. Women, one Pontiac promotional video said, "appreciate Fiero's clean, unintimidating looks."[1] No figures for how many were bought by women are available, but the car was certainly marketed heavily to them.

The Fiero hit the market in 1983, the year after the Equal Rights Amendment was definitively halted as Republicans rallied around antifeminist Phyllis Schlafly and the minimum number of states failed to ratify it. Women were nonetheless making huge strides in the workplace and in society, and the image of the independent, single woman, though still something of a novelty, was gaining currency in advertising and in the American mind.

The commercial showing a leaping female driver was followed by one for a souped-up 1985 model, where a man in a college varsity jacket hitches a ride on the side of a country road. A woman in a Fiero stops to offer him a lift, but he declines to get in as the narrator says the Fiero is a great car, but "some people want even more." A second woman in a Fiero halts and the college student again refuses a ride. Then, a narrator introduces a new, GT version of the Fiero with a V-6 engine as it comes roaring down the road with yet another woman at the wheel. This time the hitchhiker is interested. The driver slows down and looks at him over the top of her sunglasses, then roars off, leaving him in her dust by the roadside.

Fiero wasn't just an unusual car because of its plastic body and mid-body engine placement. It was unique in that it was made at GM's first plant to use manufacturing methods borrowed from the Toyota Production System, which would later be adopted as the GM manufacturing system. Pontiac had hired W. Edwards Deming, the management guru deemed responsible for improving Japanese car quality in the postwar years, as a consultant.

Though many of the methods used are now pretty standard across the global auto industry, they were groundbreaking at the time. After the oil shocks of the late 1970s and early 1980s hit the U.S. auto industry, Japanese carmakers had been gaining market share as consumers sought smaller, more fuel-efficient cars. And the Japanese were recognized as being way ahead of American manufacturers in terms of managing costs and quality. In 1984, GM even signed a joint venture agreement with Toyota to build cars at what was called the New United Motor Manufacturing, Inc. (NUMMI), on the site of a shuttered GM plant in Fremont, California, in hopes of absorbing some of the Japanese carmaker's manufacturing secrets.

It was against this background that Mary Barra began her career as a young engineer at the Fiero plant. She wanted to be part of the innovation. It was an exciting place and time, and the plant's methods were considered experimental. In her junior year at General Motors Institute (GMI), where she was sponsored by the Pontiac division and had worked inspecting Grand Prix hoods and fenders for defects, among other jobs, she applied to work at the Fiero plant. "I just thought it would be really great because it was built on all the team concepts," she says. "I wanted to be in that environment."

After graduating, she was hired onto the plant as a controls engineer, and later became the engineer responsible for plant facilities and maintenance, overseeing a team of millwrights, plumbers, sanitation workers, and electricians. Those were the guys—and virtually all of them were guys—who kept the plant clean and kept it running. "It was the first time I'd ever supervised people," she says. "We worked a lot on quality."

Located in the town of Pontiac and formerly part of GM's Fisher Body division, the plant had previously manufactured chassis for multiple Pontiac models, which were then shipped to other locations for assembly. When the company shifted to making bodies in the same plants at which cars were built, the Pontiac plant was idled. In the early 1980s, it was converted in a so-called brownfield process to build the Fiero.

The name Fiero—Italian for "proud"—was chosen by Pontiac's workers, just one of the symbols that this was going to be a cooperative effort between management and labor. The UAW agreed to labor concessions in return for more so-called teaming. It was an experimental production model based on Japanese methods that broke down the barriers between salaried managers and hourly line workers. The theory behind it was that workers on the line who actually produced cars might have good ideas about how to make them.

All employees of the plant wore the same clothes, khaki pants and T-shirts or polo shirts with their names and Fiero logos on them, rather than suits and ties for the bosses. Managers and hourly workers parked in the same parking lots (no separate spaces for executives as in other auto plants at the time), ate their meals together, and toiled on the lines together, recalls Cheri Alexander, the former head of personnel and later the plant manager. Most important, workers were consulted about plant decisions rather than simply being given orders to follow.

Barra's tasks included making sure the plant was clean and the equipment properly maintained and repaired. She spent her days walking the floor or overseeing her crews, often chatting on the two-way radio with Alexander, whose voice has the same somewhat nasal Michigander tones. They referred to themselves as "chicks on the radio," and sometimes played tricks on their coworkers who found it hard to distinguish them by voice. In retaliation, the plant manager assigned Alexander to trap a bird that had gotten into the plant and was flying around "doing its business" all over the plant. Alexander enlisted Barra's help. The pair lured the bird into a cage baited with food, then released it into the wild at a nearby lake area. "A lot of the workers were offering to kill it for us," Alexander says.

Barra says it took a while for everyone to get on board with the production system. Borrowed directly from the Japanese automakers was the plant's Andon board, which allowed workers to pull a cord to stop the assembly line when they spotted a quality problem or when a machine broke down. A musical chime would sound, with each line having its own tune.

It was a radical departure to allow line workers that much authority over the assembly line, where minutes lost could quickly translate into dollars lost. It involved trust that the workers wouldn't use the chime to get more break time, for instance.

When there was an equipment breakdown, it was Barra's team that would spring into action, to identify the problem and come up with a solution. Under such pressure, she says, it took a while to realize that rather than ask the workers "Why did you pull the cord?"

with its implied reproach, managers had to learn to say, "How can I help you?"

Barra took the teamwork approach to heart. Alexander recalls watching her on a day when the paint shop equipment failed. Not only did each minute count in terms of lost production, but the paint breakdown was even more serious than others because as time went on it could thicken to the wrong consistency and become unusable or block up machines. Alexander says Barra didn't lose her cool. Surrounded by her team of plumbers and electricians, she solicited their input until they were able to come up with a plan.

The Fiero plant had one of the highest quality rankings of any GM plant. "It was GM's best plant," says Alexander, who is now a professor of management at the University of Michigan's Ross School and teaches a case history based on the Fiero. The car also won accolades. The year of its launch, the Fiero was chosen as one of the 10 best cars of the year by *Car & Driver* magazine. The vehicle sold some 100,000 units in 1984, its first model year, making it one of Pontiac's biggest successes in more than a decade.

Right from the start, though, the Fiero had a troubling flaw. Because of its design, the car's engine had a tendency to catch fire. Connecting rods could blast through the side of the engine, causing an oil leak that could lead to a fire.[2] As horrifying as having a car's engine catch fire could be, with the Fiero the conflagrations were even more harrowing because the engine was located close to the passenger compartment and could potentially burn the car's occupants. And, because the body was made of plastic, the flames could spread quickly.

As early as 1983, GM engineers had witnessed such fires in test models. Yet, according to *Wall Street Journal* reporters Paul Ingrassia and Joseph B. White, who won a Pulitzer Prize for their coverage of the auto industry, GM was reluctant to recall the popular car. Instead, the company often treated the fires as a warranty claim, paying for repairs. The first widespread recall of Fieros took place only in December 1987, and that was ordered by the government's National Highway Traffic Safety Administration (NHTSA), following an investigation of the fires. GM recalled 125,440 cars—its entire model production for 1984. The remainder of Fieros were the subject of a second recall only in 1990, more than a year after production of the car had ceased and the plant had closed. The Fiero became "an infamous symbol of GM's corporate disease,"[3] Ingrassia and White wrote in their 1995 book, *Comeback*.

The 1987 recall was to correct conditions that could lead to the engine compartment fires. Some 260 engine fires and 22 injuries were reported by the company, according the *Detroit Free Press*.[4] The fires were recorded in about one in every five cars built that year.[5]

Viewed from today's perspective, the Fiero story bears some unsettling similarities to that of the Chevy Cobalt debacle that was to define the first months of Barra's tenure as chief executive in 2014. And the "corporate disease" that Ingrassia and White write about seems to have survived decades later, based on the criticism in a report Barra commissioned from attorney Anton Valukas about the ignition switch disaster.

As with the Fiero, GM failed to categorize the Cobalt's ignition defect as one that could injure customers. GM engineers classified the ignition flaw that could shut off the engine while someone was driving as a "customer convenience" issue. (GM's engineers apparently failed to make the connection that the loss of power that disabled power steering and power brakes could also disable the air bags.) Recalls were delayed, sometimes by years, and came only after the car in question was no longer produced. Unlike with the Fiero, though, where no deaths were reported, at least 45 customers died in cars with the faulty ignition switches, while scores more filed claims.

The fires weren't the Fiero's only problem. After its dazzling launch in 1984, sales began to decline, at first a little, then by a lot. From around 90,000 units a year in 1984 and 1985, they declined to 68,000 in 1986 and just 42,000 in 1987. The car was losing money, and GM's financial overseers wanted the bleeding stopped.[6]

Late in February 1988, Alexander got a call telling her to drive to GM's technical plant in Warren, Michigan, where a limousine was waiting to take her to downtown Detroit. Alexander had never been in a limousine before, and she had never been beyond the marble lobby of GM's headquarters offices, an Albert Kahn–designed landmark on Detroit's West Grand Boulevard. Still in her Fiero clothes, she was whisked up to the 15th floor and ushered into an executive committee meeting. After being quizzed on the details of the plant's union contract and production schedule, she was told that management had decided to close the plant down. Almost 30 years later, her eyes fill with tears as she recalls that day.

Alexander was able to find new jobs for all but about 17 of the plant's employees. Many of them wound up transferring to a new GM plant that was ramping up for production in Spring Hill, Tennessee. This plant, too, aimed at having good labor-management relations and Japanese-inspired production methods. It was launching a whole new brand of car, called Saturn.

With seven months' notice as the plant wound down its production, Barra considered what to do next in her career. As a manager with a GMI pedigree, she wasn't in danger of losing her job. But she wanted to do something more than clean up plants and repair assembly line breakdowns. She decided to apply for a General Motors Fellowship to get an MBA. The company would give her the two years off to complete her studies and would pay for her to take the courses. The only thing she had to do was get accepted to Stanford University's Graduate School of Business, one of the most selective programs in the country.

She was wait-listed.

Alexander was furious. "I called the admissions office at Stanford and told them they were ridiculous, and if they didn't accept her we were going to send her to MIT," she says. To her mind, Barra was on track to become a Sloan Fellow, a program GM had at the time to send a handful of its best rising managers to obtain an MBA at either Stanford or the Massachusetts Institute of Technology. Whether Alexander's lobbying helped or not, Barra ultimately made the cut. She headed to Silicon Valley shortly before the final Fiero rolled off the line at the plant in Pontiac. It was the last time Pontiacs were built in the town that gave the marque its name.

Of course, Barra was not yet an executive, and as head of maintenance would not have had anything to do with the decision to close the plant, or to recall the cars. For all of the plant's embrace of democratic methods, it was still the finance guys who had the final say, even though plant management and the union did make an attempt to change their minds.

Still, working there was a positive experience in the lessons it imparted, Barra says. "I learned a lot about leadership," she says, citing the emphasis on teamwork and motivating the workforce. "It was all about hearts and minds," she says. You are winning employees' loy-alty not just to be nice, she says, but "because fundamentally, you get better results if people are engaged."

As the plant was winding down production, preparing to close, the teams kept their pride in their work, ensuring that the last vehi-cles maintained the same quality as those made in the boom years. "I have a lot of respect for the leadership of the plant at the time," she says. "They got through a very difficult situation with strength and focus."

Even with all the problems of the Fiero that ultimately led GM to kill the model, "we were on the right track," Barra insists. "We just didn't put everything together well."

The lessons have stayed with her during the 2014 crisis, when GM recalled 30 million cars. "I learned that the product's got to be right, or it can have devastating consequences."

Today, there is still a mythology around the Fiero among car afi-cionados. There's a thriving Internet-based community of fans who sell parts, restore cars, and meet regularly for shows and rallies. Decades after the sexy television commercials, the sitcom *How I Met Your Mother* devoted an entire 2007 episode to a recollection of the main character's Fiero, which he had driven until it hit 200,000 miles on the odometer and broke down.

But the Fiero story didn't end with a nostalgic glow. A year and a half after the plant shut down, in January 1990, Pontiac announced that it was recalling 244,000 Fieros—every single one it had ever made—because of the fire risk.[7]

By then, Barra was already well into her second year at Stanford. The degree she earned there would give her insight into a world beyond the auto industry and shape her management style in the future. It would also put her on the fast track to move up the executive ranks when she got back to GM.

Notes

1. https://www.youtube.com/watch?v=Scd9JhaW5uY.
2. www.nytimes.com/1990/01/24/us/gm-plans-recall-of-244000-fieros-citing-f
    ire-hazard.html.

3. Paul Ingrassia and Joseph B. White, *Comeback: The Fall and Rise of the American Automobile Industry* (New York: Touchstone/Simon & Schuster, 1995), 99.

4. John Lippert, "GM to Idle Fiero Plant, Kill Model," *Detroit Free Press*, March 2, 1988, 1A.

5. Nunzio Lupo, "2 Hot Years, and Then a Burnout," *Detroit Free Press*, March 2, 1988, 1A.

6. John Lippert, "How Pontiac's Fiero Met Its End," *Detroit Free Press*, March 20, 1988, 1A.

7. www.nytimes.com/1990/01/24/us/gm-plans-recall-of-244000-fieros-citing-fire-hazard.html.

Chapter 4

Chevy Blazer: Groundbreaking Laws

"Can you ever see the day," asked Bob Stempel, "when a woman could become the CEO of General Motors?"

Stempel would later become the carmaker's CEO himself, but on the day in the late 1980s when he posed the question, he was a corporate vice president. The person being questioned was J. Michael Losh, a top manufacturing and finance executive who had been in charge of the Pontiac Motor division while Mary Barra worked at the Fiero plant. He recalls that the Detroit meeting was also attended by John Francis "Jack" Smith Jr., who would later succeed Stempel as CEO and who gave Barra one of her biggest career breaks when he hired her as his executive assistant.

The meeting was Losh's annual "progression and succession review," where he would brief his superiors on how his business was doing, and talk about the career development of the people who worked for him. Losh didn't know Barra while she worked at the Fiero plant—she was quite a few rungs below him—and by the time of this meeting she had already headed to California for her MBA. But Losh remembers well the pressure from his bosses to look for talented women like her and to help their careers advance. So do numerous other GM managers, going back at least to the 1970s.

Even in the late 1980s, very few women had made it into the executive suite. Those who did had mixed experiences. Marina von Neumann Whitman, whose father, John von Neumann, was a mathematician and scientist who helped create the atomic bomb and was known for his contributions to other fields such as economics (game theory), was recruited by Roger Smith in 1979 to be the company's vice president and chief economist. She stayed for 13 years, taking on the role of vice president in charge of external relations. Though Whitman had an illustrious career as an academic economist and had served on President Richard Nixon's Council of Economic Advisers, her advice was often ignored by GM executives, as she describes in detail in her autobiography.[1] Maureen Kempston Darkes, an attorney who joined GM's legal staff in 1975 and went on to run GM Canada and the company's overseas operations in the 1990s, recalls the loneliness of being female in the executive dining room.

By the time Barra began her GM career, the sands were beginning to shift. "The 1970s were a real tipping point," says Kathleen Gerson, a professor of sociology who studies gender and work issues at New York University. For the first time, there were more women in the labor force than out of it. Thanks in large part to the birth control pill, the birth rate dropped below the replacement rate for the first time. In addition, "this was a period of legal ferment," Gerson says, with affirmative action generally accepted as a legitimate way of redressing inequality. A series of U.S. laws had taken effect in the 1960s and 1970s that ushered in new protections for minorities and women in the workplace. Companies that continued to discriminate could lose government business, and they could also face costly lawsuits—something General Motors would learn the hard way.

Young women in the 1980s were swept up in a tide of optimism that they could do anything and that full equality was only a matter of time. "Doors were opening for women," Gerson says. "Barra was part of the first generation of women to walk through those doors."

Barra says that her parents encouraged her to follow her interest in math in college and that she never felt like she was being steered away from a technology career. Even though her parents had divided up the household chores between her and her brother along gender lines, with Barra helping her mother in the kitchen, she was allowed to follow her interest in cars and science and watch her father in his workshop after finishing her work. "I got to do what I wanted," she says.

The women's movement had begun to stir after a suburban house-wife and Smith College graduate living in New Jersey named Betty Friedan wrote *The Feminine Mystique* in 1963. The book described the boredom and dissatisfaction of educated women stuck at home out of the workforce, which Friedan dubbed "the problem that has no name." It struck a chord with thousands of housewives across the country and helped usher in the women's movement that exploded later in that decade as the baby boom generation began to reach adulthood and demand a more equitable world.

Under the Equal Pay Act, which President John F. Kennedy signed into law in June 1963,[2] wage discrimination was prohibited for men and women in the same establishment who perform jobs that require substantially equal skill, effort, and responsibility under similar working conditions. At the time, women earned less than 60 cents for every dollar earned by men. In more than 50 years since then, the so-called gender pay gap has narrowed, but it persists. In 2012, women still earned only about 77 cents for every dollar earned by men, according to the Institute for Women's Policy Research in Washington, D.C.

The Civil Rights Act of 1964 enforced the constitutional right to vote and outlawed racial segregation in schools, government offices, workplaces, and other public facilities. Thanks to Rev. Dr. Martin Luther King Jr., the whole country had been made aware of the shame-ful second-class treatment black citizens faced, particularly in the South, and public opinion favored making things right.

The act also ushered in more protections for women. While the bill was being debated on the floor of the House of Representatives, Howard Smith, a conservative Virginia Democrat who opposed inte-gration, added a provision to prohibit discrimination on the basis of sex. There is disagreement among historians as to whether Smith added the proviso in hopes of sinking the bill. If that was the case, he failed: The

Civil Rights Act was approved by Congress and signed into law by President Lyndon Johnson in July 1964.[3]

The civil rights law was followed eight years later by Title IX of the Education Amendments of 1972, which states that "no person in the United States shall, on the basis of sex, be excluded from participation in, be denied the benefits of, or be subjected to discrimination under any education program or activity receiving federal financial assistance."[4]

Title IX is generally remembered for ensuring equality of funding for sports for women, but its intent went much beyond that. Universities across the country began recruiting and enrolling large numbers of women. While Barra was attending GMI in the early 1980s, the total number of woman enrolled in higher education exceeded the number of men for the first time, a trend that has continued. (The exception is in science and engineering programs like the one Barra took, but more about that later.)

Also in 1972, Congress approved an amendment to the Constitution that was even more strongly worded and aimed at protecting women's rights. It prohibited discrimination based on sex through any rule, law, or action of the federal government. Any institution, company, or organization that got federal contracts, aid, or funds of any kind would have to comply.

The Equal Rights Amendment was passed by both houses of Congress by such a wide margin that it was widely expected to be ratified by the necessary two-thirds majority of state legislatures ahead of the 1979 deadline. This was not to be. Even after the deadline was extended until 1982, the ERA failed to receive the requisite state approvals. The amendment fell victim to a national campaign from opponents, including Phyllis Schlafly, who claimed that the ERA would usher in single-sex bathrooms and the military draft for women. Still, during the 10 years in which feminists fought for its passage, companies that did business with the government—including automakers—made sure that they would be compliant if the amendment was ratified.

Like many other large U.S. corporations, General Motors took a series of steps to comply with the new legislation. The automaker began recruiting women to attend General Motors Institute. Since its founding in 1919, GMI had graduated just one woman as of 1971. The only time the school had a large coterie of female students was during World

War II, when women were called upon to staff the country's factories while men were drafted. The school developed an engineering-
technician training course for women with college degrees. Starting in
1943, classes of women spent 15 weeks at GMI's Flint, Michigan, campus, with 48 hours a week of class, laboratory work, and supervised
study. Afterward, the women were qualified to work in either a testing laboratory or an engineering department, according to a university
brochure from the period.[5] But once the war ended, the vast majority
of the women returned home.

In 1972, GMI enrolled 27 female students. By 1980, when Barra
began studying electrical engineering there, almost a third of the students
on campus were women.

GM also began seeking women to advance in its corporate ranks. In
1973, the company asked 45,000 of its blue-collar women whether they
wanted the chance to advance, and offered training to the 2,100 who
responded affirmatively, Laurence Vickery, the company's director of
employment practices, told the *New York Times*.[6] At the time, women
made up only about 13 percent of GM's workforce of 600,000, the *Times*
reported.

Most of the new positions were low-level supervisory jobs, though.
In 1972, the highest-ranking woman at GM was a 33-year-old former
secretary named Marguerite Novelli. The manager, whose lipstick color
and outfit were described in detail in a profile in the *Detroit News*,[7] was
one of three assistant corporate secretaries at the company. Despite having the highest rank of any woman at the Big Three automakers, Novelli made less than $24,000 a year, and was not far enough up in the
GM hierarchy to be eligible for an annual bonus or even a company-
subsidized car.

The one area where women had staked a claim in Detroit was as
car designers. General Motors hired female designers to work in what
was sometimes referred to as "the beauty parlor"—officially the Art and
Color Section that the company created in 1927. "The market made
it clear that appearance was selling cars," wrote GM's legendary chief,
Alfred P. Sloan, in his 1963 memoir, *My Years with General Motors*, of the
need for selling cars in different colors and attractive styles. Sloan, who
is credited with originating many management concepts that endure to
this day, also claimed to be the first to hire women as car designers

"to express the woman's point of view. We were the first to do so, I believe, and today, we have the largest number of them in the industry."[8]

Though such views seem enlightened for their era, they didn't extend to every level of the company. Many female and minority employees felt they didn't have the same opportunities as men to advance in their careers. In 1973 General Motors and its union, the United Auto Workers, were hit with a complaint by the Equal Employment Opportunity Commission (EEOC) charging discrimination based on race and sex.

It took 10 years to resolve the lawsuit. Announced in October 1983, the out-of-court settlement was at the time the largest ever by a company in an employment discrimination case. The five-year deal was signed by then EEOC Chairman Clarence Thomas, the current Supreme Court justice who was himself famously accused of sexual harassment by Anita Hill. It called for GM to pay $42.5 million, to promote a substantial number of minorities and women into managerial jobs, and to recruit and train others. It also endowed scholarships for its employees and their children, especially members of minority groups and women, at 37 universities. Those scholarships still exist today, at campuses ranging from Alabama State to Yale University. Managers began to have the diversity of their staff included as a metric when it came time for their annual salary review.

Even before the lawsuit was settled, attitudes at the company had started to change. "The family situation 25 to 30 years ago was that when something had to be fixed—a light switch, the furnace, or the car—parents let the boys do it," Alex C. Mair, vice president of GM's technical staffs group, told *Ward's Auto World* in 1980. "Today we're looking for women who had these opportunities while growing up." One such woman was Barra.

Even among women who chose engineering as a career, that wasn't a foregone conclusion, says Karen Palmer, who was a classmate of Barra's at General Motors Institute in the early 1980s. She recalls the time when one of her sorority sisters got a flat tire; the classmate called her father to come and fix it. Palmer, the daughter and granddaughter of autoworkers who had taught her to be comfortable around cars, showed her classmates how to do it themselves.

"In the 1980s, we really began to focus on getting the right talent," says Maureen Kempston Darkes, who helped establish women's groups at the company while she headed GM Canada, and initiated a program to let corporate staff get experience working in the production plants. "We sought women coming out of engineering school." Previously, the company had hired women who had already begun their careers elsewhere, and they could have a hard time adapting to the auto industry's culture. Kempston Darkes created a program where executives could rotate into a plant for six months to get acclimated to life on the factory floor.

By 1992, about 12 percent of GM's managerial jobs were held by women, about twice the level of rivals Ford and Chrysler.[9] Still, those who made it to the top levels complained that their pay was lower than their male counterparts' pay, and that a lack of mentors and the old boys' network kept them from rising higher. And about half said that they had experienced sexual harassment on the job.

Attitudes toward harassment of the kind GMI's female students experienced on the factory floor were changing rapidly, though. "There had been a tendency of male executives to regard sexual harassment as hogwash," says Marina von Neumann Whitman. "Then, suddenly, these guys realized that their daughters were part of a whole generation of women entering the workforce." They didn't want their children treated as second-class citizens.

So when Stempel asked Losh about GM having a female CEO one day, he didn't hesitate in replying. "Of course," Losh said. "I have daughters."

Notes

1. Marina von Neumann Whitman, *The Martian's Daughter: A Memoir* (Ann Arbor: University of Michigan Press, 2013), Chapters 9 and 10.
2. www.eeoc.gov/laws/statutes/epa.cfm.
3. www.archives.gov/education/lessons/civil-rights-act/.
4. www.dol.gov/oasam/regs/statutes/titleix.htm.
5. Kettering University Archives.

6. Mary Salpukas, "G.M.'s New Deal for Women Workers," *New York Times*, February 18, 1973, 208.

7. Suzy Farbman, "Auto Women," *Detroit News Sunday Magazine*, May 14, 1972, 20.

8. Alfred P. Sloan, *My Years with General Motors* (New York: Currency/Doubleday, 1963, 1990), 272–273.

9. David J. Morrow, "Slow Road to Success," *Detroit Free Press*, December 14, 1992, 12F.

Chapter 5

Chevy Malibu: Expanding Vistas

A rriving on the Stanford University campus in the fall of 1988, Mary Barra stepped into a completely different environment. It wasn't just the palm trees and mild Pacific breezes that were a departure from the lake-dotted flats of southern Michigan. Stanford was one of the most selective programs in the country, and the Graduate School of Business class of 1990 was peopled with students from 34 states and 20 different countries. Most of the students had backgrounds in finance or general management, and many had studied at exclusive East Coast academic establishments that were nothing like the gritty, hands-on training Barra had experienced at General Motors Institute.

Stanford's business school was founded in 1926 at the instigation of alumnus Herbert Hoover, a mining engineer who became U.S. president in 1929. The school established a reputation as one of the best in the country for training good general managers using the social sciences as a framework. By 1990, the program was so much in demand that there were 4,354 applicants for the 330 places.

The faculty included luminaries such as George P. Shultz, President Ronald Reagan's secretary of state, and Myron Scholes, who went on to win a Nobel Memorial Prize in economics a few years later for his work on valuing derivatives. Women were a rarity among the faculty. Only nine of the 120 professors listed in the business school catalog were female, and fewer still had tenure. One of the first who obtained tenure was Joanne Martin, a professor of organizational behavior who is now retired. She recalls arriving at Stanford in 1977 after earning her PhD in social psychology at Harvard, and walking one day into the restroom labeled "faculty." She was faced with a row of urinals.

Barra's class included many people who went on to distinguished careers, such as Andreas Halvorsen and John Griffin, two of the so-called Tiger Cubs who worked with Tiger Management Company's legendary investor Julian Robertson and now manage hedge funds of their own. There were children of wealthy or famous people, such as Gary Lauder, grandson of cosmetics company founder Estée Lauder, who is today a Silicon Valley investor.

For a woman who had grown up in the working class in the Midwest, the new surroundings were eye-opening. "It helped you to know what you don't know," Barra says.

The 27-year-old Barra moved to the Bay area with just a couple of suitcases. Tony Barra, whom she married after graduating from GMI, stayed behind in the Detroit area, where he was building his own career. So she lived in the dorms with a roommate, and either headed back to Detroit to visit him on weekends or he would visit her. She bunked with a film major named Catherine Malcolm. Barra recalls getting to know her roommate, a Canada native who was working on a documentary about homeless people at the time, as another broadening experience. In her spare time, she ran and worked out at the school's gym.

Barra's cohort also included another GM Fellow, Ben Gibert, a rising young engineer who had also studied at GMI and who had spent the ensuing years working in product development at General Motors. He recalls how he and Barra stood out from much of the class. "Stanford was Ivy League dominated, second- and third-generation money dominated," says Gibert, an African American whose father was a chauffeur and whose mother was a domestic worker. "There were not a lot of working-class people."

While the professors were helpful and understanding, Gibert says, some classmates underestimated Barra and Gibert. "They didn't think we were very smart," he says, recalling laughing with her about it. Gibert and Barra both wound up graduating in the top 10 percent of their class.

Barra bulldozed through those attitudes. Gibert remembers getting an assignment in one class that involved working with a group of a half dozen students. As she had done as yearbook editor in Waterford Mott and in her classes at GMI, Barra took charge of the group, parceled out chores to each member, and made sure deadlines were met.

"She was like a pacer," Gibert says. "You got the assignment on Wednesday at noon, and she would set up a kickoff meeting for 5 P.M. that same day." While other students might spend the afternoon sunning themselves or shooting the breeze on the Oval, a grassy pedestrian area at the entrance to campus, Barra would hit the library and arrive at the 5 P.M. meeting with a reading list for group members and suggested assignments for each. Gibert, a mechanical engineer, might be asked to use his drafting ability and communications skills to draw up a flowchart that summarized how the assignment would be put together. Barra was good at motivating classmates to get the work done, or, failing that, to maneuver around them so that they wouldn't bring down the group.

In relaxed California, Barra's focus on work stood out. "We were from a factory environment," Gibert says. "You work a 10- or 12-hour day and you hit your deadlines."

Though the business school was known in the 1970s for its strength in finance and accounting, by the time Barra attended it was moving more toward organizational behavior subjects that drew heavily on psychology and, in large part because of its location in Silicon Valley, it was developing a specialization in the study of entrepreneurship. Barra took two classes on entrepreneurship. The classes used the case history method, but with a twist: "The great thing about those classes was you'd have a case and usually the business owner was there," Barra says. The owner would explain what he or she did and why in the particular case, and tell the class how it turned out.

Barra especially remembers a talk given by Steve Jobs while she was at the school. "He was obviously brilliant," she says. "He had the ability to look over the horizon and see how you can use technology to add value to the consumer in a way that's beautifully designed." When Barra became CEO of GM decades later, she read through many other companies' mission and vision statements to try to create a similar statement for the automaker. "When you read Apple's statement today, you can read it without the title and say, 'That's Apple,'" she says. She aimed to replicate that for GM with what she calls "who we are and why we're here."

The first year of the program consisted mainly of required courses in accounting, finance, economics, and other basic disciplines typically found in business schools. The second year was devoted to elective courses.

Barra recalls filling gaps in her own background by taking classes in subjects such as finance, statistics, and marketing. But she also signed up for classes taught by Charles Holloway, who then was a specialist in manufacturing and operations. "I took everything I could that he taught," she says.

Operations—the mechanics of running a company day to day—had only recently come back into fashion as a subject at the university. In the late 1970s and early 1980s, it had fallen so far out of favor that it was no longer even a degree requirement, according to David Kreps, who joined the faculty in the 1970s and is currently Distinguished Professor of Management. By the late 1980s, when Barra attended, it had been reinstated and today is still a required course for first-year MBA students, though it focuses on service as well as manufacturing industries.

"This was an era when the Japanese were clearly the best in the world in manufacturing," Holloway says. "The U.S. was behind." Until that time, U.S. companies had argued that to improve the quality of a product, you'd have to spend more money making it. "The Japanese demonstrated that higher quality could be achieved less expensively by designing better processes and by getting workers on the line engaged in designing the processes that would be most efficient," he says. Barra, who had worked at the Pontiac Fiero plant as it tried to adopt the Japanese manufacturing methods, had seen that firsthand and learned how difficult it would be to bring those methods to U.S. plants.

Holloway, today Stanford's Kleiner Perkins Caufield & Byers professor of management emeritus, remembers Barra well, not only because she aced his classes in manufacturing strategy and new product and process development, but also because her background in the auto industry was unusual. "Many of the students at Stanford came from consulting backgrounds, which means you talk about things," rather than make them, he says. Other students came from financial backgrounds and were focused mainly on costs. Barra's manufacturing background "fed directly into my own interests"—designing and manufacturing things. Holloway had just returned from a yearlong sabbatical at MIT and Harvard, where he'd done research on product and process development.

How unusual was a manufacturing background at Stanford in those days? Professor Myra Strober, a labor economist who taught at both the school of education and the business school at the time, recalls giving students in a labor relations class at the business school a case history dealing with union grievances. The grievance involved a manufacturer that wasn't allowing its workers to go to the bathroom during their shifts. When the students started discussing the case, she realized that they had little concept of what it was like to actually work on the factory floor. So she asked them who had ever been inside a factory. Not one hand was raised. She arranged a field trip to a plant just across the San Francisco Bay from the Stanford campus: It was New United Motor Manufacturing, Inc. (NUMMI), the joint venture between GM and Toyota. (NUMMI wasn't the subject of the case history.)

Barra also stood out in Holloway's classes for another reason. "She was completely capable of holding her own against the men," he says. Though a quarter of the MBA student body was female, there were only five or six women in each of Holloway's classes of about 60 students.

His classes also took the form of case studies, written about specific business problems. At times, Holloway brought in executives of the companies being studied. One speaker was Ford Motor Company's Donald Peterson, the first CEO in the company's history who wasn't a member of the founding Ford family, who talked about how to build a culture of collaboration in the auto industry. At one point in his career, Peterson had been assigned to Ford's truck division, which was considered a dead end for managers whose careers weren't going any further.

In the absence of pressure to jockey for career advancement, Peterson and the other truck managers began to collaborate, and began sharing ideas on how to make better trucks. They did that so well that the truck division began making money and Peterson was eventually elevated to CEO of Ford. Trucks still account for a huge slice of profits at U.S. automakers, including GM.

Professors relied on student discussions to bring out the points they wanted to make. "Whenever I was having trouble getting information out of the students, I would call on Mary," Holloway says. "She was very confident and knowledgeable, and she could give her thoughts in a very nonthreatening manner." Barra was usually not telling the class how things were done in GM, but was making comments that applied to the case being studied based on her own experience.

Eugene Tan, who took several classes with Barra, remembers her for similar reasons. "A lot of the women in our class were a bit shy," he says. "She wasn't afraid to get up and say what she thought."

Students overall were friendly and willing to help each other out, male or female. Tan, who had studied accounting as an undergraduate in Hong Kong, says he held informal cram courses in the subject for some students. The grades went from H for honors, then P+, P, and P−, all of which were passing grades. "There wasn't really that heavy competition between the students that you see in some schools," he says.

Married students, such as Barra, tended to socialize separately from the singles, who had more parties and outings. But almost everyone would get together after class on Fridays for the "liquidity preference function," a sly reference to John Maynard Keynes's macroeconomic equation about calculating the demand for money. Only in this case, the liquid was either beer or wine, often donated by the school or a business sponsor that might have sent a speaker, and the function took place in a courtyard on campus next to the business school.

When Barra attended, the curriculum was shifting from traditional management topics to include more topics involving organizational behavior, which had a big dose of psychology. The students jokingly referred to one such course as "touchy-feely." Former students recall that this course included a field trip to the woods where classmates did bonding exercises, role play, and the trust game, where one person falls and relies on the group to catch him or her. Barra, who didn't take the course, now says she wishes she had because the lessons about how to inspire and lead employees would have been useful at General Motors.

Operations once again has become a hot topic at the business school, but for different reasons than in the 1980s. In the new economy typified by computer makers such as Hewlett-Packard and Apple Computer Inc., companies are designing and marketing innovative products but outsourcing their manufacture to third parties, often companies based overseas. Supply chain management has become an important topic because companies need to ensure that these suppliers are delivering the parts they need to their specifications and of the quality required.

Holloway says the subject applies not just to computer makers, but is also important for carmakers like GM, which no longer make every part of their vehicles but create them with outsourced components in assembly plants.

It was an outside supplier, Delphi Automotive, that made the ignition switch blamed for crashes of the Chevy Cobalt and other models that have resulted in at least 45 deaths (although Delphi was previously part of GM until being spun off in 1999, several years before the switch began being produced). According to the independent report GM commissioned on the affair in 2014, the switches were approved for use in the vehicles even though they failed to meet the company's specifications. So better supply chain management, in theory, might have prevented that switch from being used.

Barra also had a real-life case study in how people react in a disaster while at Stanford, when the 1989 earthquake struck San Francisco, killing 63 people. "We were in class, and it was being taped because we had a guest speaker," she says. Then came the loud rumbling of the quake. Watching the tape later, she said, "you could see everybody just bolt." Though traditional advice is to shelter under a desk, students in the classroom 10 steps below ground level ran out to into the open, she says, where "you could literally see cement sidewalks rippling."

Barra's former classmates took bragging rights when she was named GM's CEO. "She is our shining star," declares Izumi Kabayashi-Yaskawa. Tan says, "I think we all sent her congratulations when she was named CEO." Tan told her about his high-school-age daughter, who was skeptical that her father really knew the woman who was going to run General Motors. When Barra heard that, she wrote directly to his daughter, he says, and encouraged her not to shy away from the hard courses in school and to consider a career in the sciences.

Barra today sits on Stanford's 65-member advisory council with other alumni, including Texas investor Robert Bass and Michelle Clayman, the money manager who endowed Stanford's Clayman Institute for Gender Studies. The council helps the school set its strategic goals and advises on curriculum. In May 2014, Barra returned to the campus where she had earned the degree that helped catapult her career. Only this time, she was the one giving lessons to Stanford business school students about leadership and how to manage people.

Barra also contracted with her alma mater to create a management training program for General Motors that is based on one that the company used to offer when she was a rising manager. The first class began shortly after she took over as CEO. "I want to create a Silicon Valley mind-set in Detroit," she says.

Chapter 6

Buick Skylark: A View from the Top

One morning in 1997, Mary Barra got an odd telephone message—the chief executive officer of General Motors, Jack Smith, wanted to interview her for a position as his assistant.

"I thought it was a joke," recalls Barra. She didn't reply to the message, and left the light blinking on her answering machine. Later in the day, she called her boss, Ken Varisco, over and played it for him. Come on, she asked him, who is trying to trick me?

He looked sheepish and apologized. "I didn't get a chance to talk to you about this yet," he said. "You'd better return that call."

Barra had returned to GM from Stanford to a job that was less than her dream role, as a senior staff engineer in operations services for what was then the Chevy-Pontiac-Canada group. Essentially, it was another facilities management job, not too far removed from the post she'd held at the Fiero plant.

She let her boss know that she wanted something that would involve working more with the cars themselves rather than plant facilities. "It was great that I had a frank conversation with my manager," she recalls, "but I didn't get what I wanted right away." And, she adds, "You've still got to do a good job at the job you have."

Barra spent almost three years in the maintenance role before she came to Varisco's attention. Then the director of manufacturing staff, Varisco had attended a meeting where Barra gave a presentation at GM's tech center in Warren, Michigan, about 15 miles north of Detroit. Varisco was impressed by her knowledge and especially her comfort with the corporate environment. "This was not necessarily always true of people transferring into headquarters from our plants," he says.

He hired Barra as manager of manufacturing planning for the mid-sized car division, which, after one of the company's numerous reorganizations, was in charge of building models ranging from the Chevy Cavalier to the Oldsmobile Cutlass, among others. Barra was based at the tech center in Warren, which houses the company's car designers as well as its manufacturing staff. Designed by modernist architect Eero Saarinen and a National Historic Landmark, the center is a sprawling 330-acre expanse of multicolor brick buildings and artificial lakes, studded with a silver dome and silver water tower. The center has a retro science fiction feel, so much so that it was featured recently in the *Transformers* movie series starring robots that convert into Chevrolet cars. Barra spent about half of her time at the center and the rest on the road, visiting assembly plants that were preparing to make new models, and reviewing engineering plans.

The manufacturing group reported up to Don Hackworth, a vice president, who was keenly concerned with keeping costs down and improving efficiency at GM's plants. The company was suffering from declining market share and increasing red ink. GM had lost a staggering $23.5 billion in 1992, a record for any American company at the time.[1] In an unheard-of coup, the company's board of directors had fired its chief executive, Robert Stempel, and replaced him with Smith.

One day, Hackworth met with Varisco to review how well the factories were doing at putting new car models into production. Making a new car was a massive undertaking, and the assembly plants would have to shut down to retool, adjusting the dies and other manufacturing machinery to the different model. The cost could be huge, depending on the amount of time the changeover took and the number of bugs that had to be worked out. The results varied widely from launch to launch. "At one point, Don asked me if there was a common process to launch a new product in our assembly plants," Varisco says. "I had to tell him that there was not."

After the meeting, Varisco sat brooding in his office and Barra walked in. She asked why he was upset, since he wasn't responsible for the individual plants. Varisco said that their group was responsible for providing all of the plants with efficient processes for making the cars. Barra seized the idea: "So let's do that."

Over the next months, she worked with Varisco to develop a standardized system for retooling that could be used by all of the company's plants. By using the same methods everywhere, they could increase efficiency by reducing mistakes, thereby saving time and money. They proposed organizing a separate product manufacturing staff that would parachute into plants when they were converting to a new product and manage the whole process based on the company-wide best practices.

Getting the new system adopted would be tricky, though: Up until that point, each plant manager had decided by himself how to retool, and many of them would be loath to give up their independence to a central authority. "It was a departure from the fiefdom-type environment," Varisco says. "That was a big change for a corporation our size."

Knowing that Barra shared credit for the new system and wanting to raise her visibility in the company, he let her be the one to present the idea to Hackworth and other top managers. They approved it.

The first car to be launched using the new system, an all-new Pontiac Grand Prix, was built at an assembly plant in Fairfax, Kansas. "It was the most successful launch we had ever done," Varisco says.

After that, he proposed promoting Barra, who was ranked as an eighth-level manager under GM's system, to the executive level, where she'd be eligible for an annual bonus. The promotion required a lot of supporting paperwork, including the reasons for the move and a theoretical career path. Barra had talked frequently with Varisco about her desire to get closer to actually making cars. "Her roots were in the assembly plant," he says. "You get more satisfaction there for the results that you put forth. In headquarters, you can work your butt off, but see no results for a really long time."

Varisco thought Barra should work toward becoming a plant manager, where she could put both her engineering background and her managerial skills to work. In his human resources (HR) report, he recalls writing that Barra could rise to become a vice president of manufacturing someday, or even, if she really excelled, company president (GM presidents had traditionally come from an engineering background). "I guess I sold her a bit short," he says, with wry irony.

Whether it was because of Varisco's glowing review, Hackworth's recognition of her role in creating the new product launch system, or her MBA from Stanford, Barra's name began appearing near the top of the so-called high-potential lists that the company's human resources department keeps. That led to the interview with Jack Smith and his deputy, Vice Chairman Harry Pearce.

Under Smith, a native of Massachusetts who had come up through the finance side of the company, GM was undergoing a period of great ferment. One of Smith's claims to fame was that he had negotiated the company's contract with Toyota to create the NUMMI joint venture in the 1980s. He also was credited for turning around a number of the company's loss-making international operations, including those in Europe. He pioneered the company's push into emerging markets, especially China, which today is the single largest source of sales for GM.

By the time Barra was summoned to his office in 1997, GM had returned to profitability. Smith, who was no relation to his predecessor Roger Smith, also was focused on changing the mind-set of the company, which he found bureaucratic and inward-looking. He eliminated overlapping responsibilities and cut out layers of management that had been in place since the time of Alfred P. Sloan, the company's former president and chairman from the 1920s until 1946.[2] He also moved GM's headquarters from an ornate, 1920s-era Alfred Kahn–designed building on West Grand Boulevard to the Renaissance Center (called the RenCen for short), seven round black glass towers that stand like stacks of poker chips overlooking the Detroit River. He moved GM staff from 17 locations around the area into the center, where all of GM's floors, except for the executive suite, were designed in exactly the same layout.

Jack Smith chose as his vice chairman Pearce, a former product liability litigator for GM and other automakers, who had joined the company in 1985 as associate general counsel, and who also held an engineering degree. Pearce shared Smith's desire to overhaul the company's culture. Marina von Neumann Whitman, who left the company just before Smith took over from Bob Stempel, recalls in her autobiography that Pearce had compiled a "black book" of anonymous interviews with 30 of the company's top executives that contained "devastatingly candid" assessments of the company's culture and recommendations for how to improve it. The book never made it into Stempel's hands, she writes, because a senior executive quashed it.[3] With Smith as CEO, he had a ready ear.

Smith made some small-scale changes in the executive suite, too. He decided that he and his vice chairman would share support staff, rather than have an aide for each. Until then, the executive assistants had always been drawn from the financial side of the business. By sharing the staff, the top brass could have one number cruncher and one person with knowledge of the operating side of the business. Barra, following her time at Stanford, was on the list of operations candidates.

The assistant's job wasn't just to support the boss; it was to learn the ropes about how the business was run at the highest levels and across the firm. Those chosen for the job were young people on the fast track to the top. The program was not advertised, and employees couldn't apply for the position. The point was to bring people who were maybe 10 years into their career with the company and would have seen only a very narrow part of it—engineering, finance, or purchasing, say—to the CEO's office for a year or two so that they could understand the bigger picture and move on to more important roles.

"It was a really great job for exposure to the company," says Mary Sipes, another rising executive who succeeded Barra in the assistant role, starting in 1999. She is now the company's vice president of global portfolio planning, helping to figure out how and when new products and features will be launched.

Both Smith and Pearce interviewed Barra in 1997. "She stood out," Pearce recalls. "Very easy to talk to, very engaging, not a big ego, real thirst for knowledge." Smith, who declined to be interviewed for this book, agreed with Pearce's assessment, and Barra got the job. She transferred to the executive suite on the 15th floor of GM headquarters in downtown Detroit, just down the hall from Smith and Pearce.

Though in theory Barra worked for both the CEO and the vice chairman, in practice she spent most of her time working with Pearce. "We were in and out of each other's offices all day long," Pearce says. "I literally let her follow me around to see what I did and get exposed to the issues I was dealing with on a day-to-day basis."

Pearce was responsible for all of the parts of the company that weren't cars—as well as legal and safety issues. In those days, the company was highly diversified following a buyout spree by Roger Smith in the 1980s, making everything from satellite systems to tanks to locomotives. Barra, still in her mid-30s, got to sit in on board meetings of Hughes Electronics Corporation, the defense company, and General Motors Acceptance Corporation (GMAC), the company's auto finance arm. GMAC, today called Ally Corporation, was expanding from auto finance into insurance and home mortgages and banking—businesses that would weigh down the automaker in the years leading up to its 2009 bankruptcy. Barra got firsthand exposure to what a board of directors wants in a company's management, to corporate governance guidelines, and to how big corporate decisions are made. And, since she was able to interact on a daily basis with the highest-ranking executives in the company, not just Pearce and Smith, she became known as an up-and-comer to all of GM's senior management.

Barra embraced the opportunity to broaden her experience. "She didn't have the characteristic automotive mind-set—that all you worry about is the systems in the vehicle," Pearce says. He used her to go out and talk to engineers at the company to get them on board with incorporating safety systems such as OnStar in more vehicles. OnStar, which connects drivers with a service center that can flag breakdowns or other issues, was introduced shortly before Barra joined the CEO's office. Run by Rick Wagoner, who would later become CEO, the company combined then-novel global positioning system (GPS) technology from Hughes Electronics, customer call center services from Electronic Data Systems (the H. Ross Perot company that GM owned at the time), and the company's own car engineering prowess. At first, engineers were less than enthused, Pearce says. "They'd say, 'Why do you want all that stuff in a car?'"

Pearce was also in charge of new technology, an area where he found Barra to be an enthusiastic supporter. Among the technologies the company was working on at the time was a light hybrid truck using fuel cells, for which Barra was Pearce's point person. The company was also developing a hybrid passenger car that was a precursor to the Chevrolet Volt and was testing autonomous technology—something that automakers are only now starting to roll out in models for sale to the public.

"We worked on a host of things," Barra says. "There was a lot of seeding that went on—helping people understand why something's important instead of just saying 'Jack said do this,' or 'Harry said do that.'" Pearce recalls using Barra as a go-between to the engineering staffs, whose language she spoke well.

Barra also began using her business school skills to help Pearce rationalize the various corporate staffs that he was in charge of: public policy, government relations, legal, and communications. "I became a de facto business manager," she says. "Harry wanted to drive more budget discipline and accountability."

In practical terms, that meant reviewing the tasks done by those staffs, and trying to eliminate superfluous ones or to hire outside contractors to do certain routine jobs. "Nobody ever really went in and said, 'What should you be doing to add value?'" he says. They reduced costs by a third by hiring an outsider to collect accounts payable and issue payroll checks, for instance. Barra's job was to find those kinds of opportunities, he says.

Pearce relied on Barra even more in 1998, when he was diagnosed with leukemia and was suddenly out of the office for almost six months for treatment. At the time, the recovery rate from the disease was 14 percent, he says. "She didn't miss a beat," recalls Pearce, who has since recovered. "She continued all the initiatives with the staffs and kept the pressure on in some of the advanced technology initiatives. She wanted to make sure that these things weren't going to die."

Barra also worked on a project that was closer to her personally: creating a support system for women at the company. More than 15 years after its Equal Employment Opportunity Commission (EEOC) settlement and a decade after Michael Losh was asked about a future woman CEO, General Motors still had no internal organization that women could turn to for mentoring or career advice. The company hired Catalyst, the New York–based group that studies and aims to improve opportunities for women in the workplace, to conduct a survey of its attitudes and practices toward women. CEO Jack Smith, who later became the chairman of Catalyst, supported the initiative.

GM got less than perfect marks. "You kind of found people who were still learning," Barra says mildly. "And then you have people where they had daughters who were my age or who were entering the workforce and had a keen interest in understanding how to be inclusive."

Barra felt one of the best ways to get attention for women's issues such as work/family balance and flexible hours was to make them relevant to both sexes. "One of the results, even at that time in the mid-1990s, was a lot of the issues women faced, so did men," she says. Barra helped select a group of 35 women leaders across the company who then brought the study's results to senior management. "They talked about what they saw as issues and challenges," she says. Barra, who was several months pregnant at the time, went to the staff of each member of what was then called the President's Council, or the senior leaders of the company.

One result of the study was that the company began to create so-called affinity groups for women and minorities. Maureen Kempston Darkes, one of the company's highest-ranking women at the time, led the program in Canada, and Barra was involved in the United States. "We thought there was a huge responsibility for senior women to help other women develop," Barra says. The groups held different sessions on mentoring, networking, and career development. "We'd do a 'dress for success' every year and it was hugely popular," she says.

The affinity groups morphed into what are now called "employee resource groups" in corporate-speak, and were the topic of a how-to guidebook Catalyst produced in 1999.[4] In the United States, the successor to the group Barra created is now known as GM WOMEN, which stands for "women offering mentoring, expertise, and networking." With 1,700 members, it does work similar to that done 15 years ago, with regular career planning sessions and guest speakers. The group's current president, Charlie Gandy-Thompson, is a computer engineer and 20-year veteran of the company who travels to engineering conventions to recruit talented graduates in addition to her day job at the technical center in Warren, where she's in charge of ensuring that electronic car components meet the company's standards.

Barra also helped Pearce come up with a way of improving recruiting so that GM could bring in more high-potential women and minorities as they graduated from college. "We had hiring and recruiting processes that didn't access those populations," he says. Having a diverse pool of employees is important not just for moral reasons; it also makes good business sense. "Don't you think customers pay attention when they see the senior management team and it's all white and male?" he asks.

Part of the plan involved just changing where and how the company recruited. Howard University, the historically black college located in Washington, D.C., has a very good engineering and technology program. But the school had never been on GM's list of places to recruit. That changed.

The company had been trying to increase the number of women and minorities in its ranks ever since the 1982 EEOC agreement. Smith and Pearce intensified that, making diversity one of the criteria that managers were judged on. "We even tied it to compensation," Pearce says. Cheri Alexander, who worked in human resources, says, "There was always the question: Where are the women?"

HR would review the demographics of the candidate pool any time a job opening came up. "If there was a deficiency, you'd have to explain," says Varisco, who joined the company in 1966 and saw the system come in gradually. It was a manager's responsibility to find a diverse candidate pool and to make sure he or she was developing women and minorities and not just "good ol' boys." But he says he never had to advance someone who wasn't qualified for a position, because he worked on having a pool of qualified women and minorities in his group.

Starting in the late 1980s and early 1990s, women like Barra who were identified as having high potential early on were placed on the same fast track as promising male executives. Among those her age, a couple dozen were in this role, says Annette Clayton, who got her start at a GM truck plant in Dayton, Ohio, and ultimately became president of the company's Saturn division and a vice president in charge of quality. "GM realized that women were making a lot of decisions about which cars were bought, and that its design teams and leadership didn't reflect that," Clayton says. "There was a social imperative, but more important was that it was a business imperative."

The fast track for these women was literally fast: Instead of the normal three to five years in a post, they were accelerated through different jobs every 18 to 24 months. Ben Gibert, Barra's classmate at Stanford, had a similar trajectory as a promising minority engineer before he was headhunted away by a rival automaker, one of many high-potentials who left the company. Clayton wound up joining Dell Computer in 2006 after a headhunter called, and today she is the executive vice president of Schneider Electric, in charge of the global supply chain and based in Hong Kong.

Among the women of roughly Barra's age who stayed, a robust handful are now near the pinnacle of the company. Barra says she continued to use the employee resource groups as a sounding board as she climbed the ladder, having them come in and speak with her, for instance, about racial or gender diversity while she was running global product development prior to being named CEO. "When we went through the restructuring [the 2009 bankruptcy], it kind of stopped," she says. "One of the changes we made recently is that the executive leadership team—my team—is also the diversity council and we have that as a regular agenda item."

The groups also help the staff to have a dialogue about work/life balance, Barra says. It wasn't until after the bankruptcy that the company really began to accept that people could be efficient by telecommuting or working flexible hours. "You have to let people balance and, frankly, they'll give you more," Barra says.

She learned that firsthand. During her years working for Pearce and Smith, Barra had both of her children, a boy and a girl, about one year apart. She took a maternity leave of eight weeks each time, and made sure she wrapped up as much work as possible before departing. Her fellow executive assistant, finance whiz Rick Winkley, took on some of her workload while she was gone, she says. "It was actually a great job to have" while having children, Barra says with a chuckle, because there was little worry that Smith and Pearce wouldn't have the needed support. "If the CEO needs something, you *know* it's going to get done."

Barra, too, had some struggles with figuring out how to balance career and family. Varisco recalls that she stopped by to talk to him frequently about her career path after she had moved to the RenCen. One time, she was pregnant with her first child. She was worried about how she would handle her family obligations if she were to meet one of the career goals they had discussed: becoming the manager of an auto assembly plant. "A plant manager is a 24/7 job," Varisco says. "Some of those plants work two or three shifts, and if anything happens, you have to be there." He told Barra that he thought she could successfully handle both family and career, and that the latter would only be limited by her own commitment to it.

Ultimately, Barra hired a live-out nanny to care for her children while they were small. She almost apologizes as she explains that she was fortunate to be able to afford the help, as her husband was traveling a lot for his career and her own hours could be unpredictable. She wasn't to get her plant manager job until several years later. First, she was going to step outside her comfort zone again to take on a role completely different from anything she'd done at GM before.

Notes

1. Donald W. Nauss, "GM Sets Record with 1992 Loss of $23.5 Billion: Autos," *Los Angeles Times*, February 12, 1993.
2. www.sloan.org/about-the-foundation/who-was-alfred-p-sloan-jr/.
3. Marina von Neumann Whitman, *The Martian's Daughter: A Memoir* (Ann Arbor, MI: University of Michigan Press, 2013), 263.
4. Catalyst Inc., *Creating Women's Networks: A How-To Guide for Women and Companies* (San Francisco: Jossey-Bass, 1998).

Chapter 7

Oldsmobile Intrigue: Hearts and Minds

I n the summer of 1998, General Motors was hit by the longest strike it had faced since the 1930s. Workers at the metal-stamping factory in Flint, where Mary Barra had attended college, walked off the job on June 5, 1998, and stayed off for almost two months. The plant employed just 9,000 workers—a tiny fraction of the company's North American employees—but they made parts for all of GM's factories in the United States and Canada. Their strike shut down all of GM's assembly plants across the country, idling some 200,000 workers. At issue was new equipment for the plant and the union's perception that the company reneged on a promise to give it more work.

"In the middle '90s, there was a real attitude from GM that they weren't going to communicate with us very much, and they were going to do whatever the hell they wanted," UAW Vice President Cal Rapson told *Automotive News* 10 years later.[1] His GM counterpart, Don Hackworth, told *Automotive News* that the plant's workers "didn't want to give a fair day's work and ignored warnings that inefficiency would have consequences."

The strike cost GM $2.8 billion in profit that year.

Wounds from the strike were still fresh when GMI-trained engineer Gary Cowger was called back that November from a stint in Europe, where he'd overseen manufacturing and been in charge of Opel, to take over global labor relations. In preparation for the following year's UAW contract negotiations, he thought that the company needed to repair its relationship with the union. One of the reasons the workers had struck was that they didn't fully understand the competitive pressures the company was facing.

Many in the union seemed stuck in the mind-set that had afflicted top executives a decade earlier, when Marina von Neumann Whitman grew frustrated with trying to get GM leaders to realize that the competitive landscape was changing because of Japanese competition and a recession. "It was a head in the sand culture," she says. Executives in the 1980s thought that their "natural" market share was 50 percent and that things would soon "get back to normal."

But "normal" no longer existed. GM's managers had become painfully aware of this in the early 1990s, when the company came perilously close to bankruptcy. (GM's market share has continued to shrink, falling to about 17 percent today.[2]) "We were the high-cost producer," Cowger says. But how were they to get that message across to hourly workers who believed that the company was just trying to squeeze concessions out of them?

Cowger thought the perfect person for the assignment would be Barra. Her background working in plants and manufacturing meant she knew how to talk to workers as well as to corporate managers. And she understood the jobs they did and how they fit into the overall picture. "I was impressed with how smart she was," Cowger says. "She's got terrific judgment and she's very consistent." Besides, she had been working for a couple of years with Pearce and Smith, and as a high-potential executive, she was due for a rotation into a new assignment. "These people would get reviewed more frequently," Cowger says, "and we tried to give them a varied experience."

Barra was flummoxed at the idea of taking on communications. "At first, when they talked to me about that job, I was, like, 'I'm an *engineer!*'"

she says. "But it was actually one of the big learning opportunities of my career."

How communications works was only part of what she had to learn. The biggest change from her engineering and corporate duties was that she was now working in an area where the results would be subjective. In engineering and operations, she says, "generally, you have a problem and you solve it. You solve for X, and you find the answer and there's not a lot of debate about what the answer is. What I learned in communications is that some of the most important things you do can't be quantified with an equation."

No matter how good the choices you make, "you never know: If you did something else, could it have been even more successful?" she says.

Until that point, communications at factory level had consisted of newsletters filled with the scores of the plant bowling league and news about volunteering or other charitable activities. "We were all over the place" in terms of communications, recalls Diana Tremblay, who at the time was working in labor relations. "You got very focused on your individual plant issues and not really tying it in to what the company wanted to do overall."

One of the lessons of the strike, Barra says, was: "Our employees didn't have a good understanding of the fundamentals of the business."

Barra changed that quickly. She put a communications professional into each plant, which in itself was a change; previously the role had been filled on an ad hoc basis by whoever wanted to do it, usually the local HR person. Barra charged the communicators with reporting to the workers how the plant was doing on a variety of measures. She drew on her experience in creating manufacturing processes to set up a system for communicating with workers that could be replicated from plant to plant. "She applied an engineering mind-set to communications," says one former executive.

Barra says the challenge with communications was that "Everyone has an opinion and everyone thinks they know how to do it." As a result, "you sometimes took more criticism than you ever would in an engineering or operations type function."

She put in place a system that aimed to reduce subjectivity. Each plant's results would be presented in a scorecard whose categories she can rattle off even 15 years later: SPQRCE. The unpronounceable acronym with an echo of city of Rome's motto (S.P.Q.R.) stands for safety, people, quality, responsiveness, cost, and environment. "There are metrics in each of those categories," she says.

In plants, each rest station had a screen where a line's output and metrics would be displayed. E-mail wasn't used much for hourly workers who spent their days on the factory floor without any access to a computer. Printed weekly newsletters were also used.

Close to 100 new communications people were hired at the time to ensure that all plant employees attended regular meetings where they could hear managers talk about goals and could ask questions. Juli Huston-Rough, who joined the Saginaw Metal Casting plant in 2000, recalls that some meetings began at 5 A.M. to accommodate the different shifts of workers who were operating the plant around the clock. Her team created a quality tutorial modeled after the *Jeopardy* television game show, giving out prizes such as T-shirts. "We made it fun," she says.

The communications teams also had a scorecard, which set out the number of times executives needed to meet with their plants each week, month, and quarter. The scorecards also laid out specific content for the meetings, such as discussing the plant's cost and quality metrics in relation to other plants. The idea was to say, "Hey, how are we doing as a plant? Where do we rank from a safety, quality, cost perspective? It was very disciplined," Barra says.

Not everyone was a fan of such systems, particularly in areas such as marketing and public relations. Scorecards and metrics were sometimes used so much at the company that employees could lose sight of the big picture, says Bob Lutz, who joined General Motors in 2001 as product development chief, just after Barra had moved to her next position. Lutz, the quintessential "car guy," known for his eye for groundbreaking designs, recalls how one of his subordinates approached him to ask for an extra bonus for his team. The executive brandished a scorecard in which every box was shaded green, to show that the team had met all of its metrics. "How are the cars selling?" Lutz asked. "They're not selling at all well," the executive replied.

Still, in Barra's case, the metrics seem to have served their purpose. They got white-collar workers as well as factory staff to focus more on business results and how their jobs contributed to them. GM still uses her system today in communicating with plants, though with fewer communications people. And there were no more strikes until 2007, when the company was sliding toward bankruptcy.

By 2001, Barra was on the move again. This time she was rotated back into the operations side of the business. Still working for Cowger, she was named executive director of competitive operations engineering. The long title really meant that she was tasked with helping Cowger institute the company's version of Japanese lean manufacturing methods. In a way, it was a continuation of her "hearts and minds" campaign on the communications team—only this time she needed to convince engineers to adopt some of the manufacturing methods that the company had started testing almost two decades earlier, while she was at the Fiero plant. It was one step closer to what she had told Ken Varisco half a dozen years earlier that she wanted to do: run a plant.

Her corporate overseers meanwhile kept an eye on Barra and other so-called high-potential executives who were now about to hit their 40s. Barra was tapped, along with a few dozen others, to take part in the senior executive program—a new training program set up by Rick Wagoner, a protégé of Jack Smith's who had taken over as CEO in 2000 while Smith remained as chairman. A rising star at the company, Wagoner, then just 47, was a former CFO with an MBA from Harvard who wanted to instill more business-school-style rigor into the executive ranks without having to send people off to Stanford or MIT for two years.

For the high-potential executives, the senior executive program was a sort of corporate coming out. Many of them had been mentored and coached over the years, and had known because of the size of their paychecks or bonuses as well as the number of new jobs thrust upon them that they were being groomed for bigger things, but most were never officially told that they were high potentials.

Now, they were sitting in a room with about 30 of their peers drawn from different parts of the company and from all over the world. For three one-month stints, the group worked almost around the clock, eating together, staying in hotels, and going home only every other weekend for those in the area. "It was a crash-course MBA," recalls Tony Cervone, who was in Barra's class, and now is the company's senior vice president for communications. "We took accounting, economics, marketing. They brought in Clay Christensen from Harvard, and professors from Northwestern and Duke." Christensen is a Harvard Business School management professor who specializes in innovation.

Besides Cervone, other high potentials in the class included Grace Leiblein, who went on to lead the company in Latin America and now is corporate vice president in charge of global quality; Larry Zahner, who retired in 2014 after heading manufacturing; Diana Tremblay, the vice president for global business services; and Jim Bovenzi, who went on to head the company's Russian operations.

Many of the sessions focused on case histories or included lectures from the top executives of the company, including Wagoner and Smith. But in one memorable exercise, the group split into teams, each of which had to run a widget-manufacturing business. One of the participants recalls an actual mock assembly line with pulleys and wheels, where things would go wrong and the teams would have to figure out the cause and fix it. Despite the fun nature of the exercise, which went on for several days, there were winners and losers, based on the profit and loss statement each team produced. "Everyone in that room was so damn competitive," Cervone says.

Another of the sessions involved travel to one of GM's overseas locations, in either Europe, South America, or Asia. Barra's group traveled together to Japan, where they were able to see the Toyota Production System in operation on its home turf. The future CEO Fritz Henderson, who then was running GM's operations in Japan, met with them.

They also spent two weeks in China, which was just starting to become a market for GM after Smith's push into the country. The group did some touristy things, such as visiting the Great Wall, guided by class member Larry Zahner, who was based in China at the time. But most of the time was spent helping the future leaders understand consumer habits in the world's largest market. An executive from LM Ericsson, the Swedish cell phone company, explained how Chinese consumers were skipping landlines and going right to cell phones. Cervone says the executives spent time in local people's homes. "We were given some renminbi and sent to the market to purchase and bargain for things," he says. "The natural way of doing things there was to barter for everything, even groceries. You begin to understand how a communist nation could be so capitalist."

The best part of the program, participants agreed, was simply getting to know rising stars from different parts of the company around the world. Grace Leiblein, who had attended General Motors Institute (GMI) at about the same time as Barra but hadn't met her because they were in different sections, hit it off with the future CEO. "I really liked her," says the Los Angeles native. "We have similar backgrounds and styles and we became friends in that class." Leiblein and Barra started socializing together with their husbands, both of whom also attended GMI.

Each participant left with a roster of new names of top people around the company they could call if the need arose. Cervone says that when he was transferred to Zurich he relied on Tremblay, who was later based in Antwerp, Belgium, to fill him in on issues affecting the company in Europe.

Barra also found that aspect of the training to be exceptional. "Although it was quite a while ago, there are still people that to this day … you leverage to solve problems," she says. "I thought it was outstanding."

So much so that she has relaunched the program, which stopped around the time of GM's bankruptcy, once again, this time customized by Stanford for GM. The first group of 30 or so executives, drawn from a variety of countries and backgrounds, began with a course at the Renaissance Center addressed by Barra over the summer of 2014, then had a session in China, one more back at the Renaissance Center, then a final one at Stanford. "There is a difference in Silicon Valley where a lot of innovation occurs—a lot of entrepreneurship," she says, and tells the story of a GM engineer who needed to design how to place 10 air bags into the Chevy Sonic, and was struggling for a solution. "He actually dreamt it, woke up in the middle of the night, sketched it out, then went back to bed. We have engineers that are that passionate," she says. "I really want to infuse that back. There's no reason why the Silicon Valley mind-set can only be in Silicon Valley."

Notes

1. David Barkholtz, "A Painful Lesson: Flint Strike Showed Labor-Relations Model Had to Change," *Automotive News*, September 14, 2008.
2. GM earnings report, October 23, 2014.

Chapter 8

Buick LeSabre: Fixing Hamtramck

A low, sprawling building painted a putty-yellow color, General Motors' Hamtramck assembly plant sits on a crumbling, weed-lined service road off the Edsel Ford Freeway. The plant has the unusual distinction of being located both in the confines of the independent city of Hamtramck (pronounced Ham-TRAM-ick), an enclave of 22,000 people, and the city of Detroit. Plant officials joke that workers ask to be assigned to lines on the Hamtramck end of the plant, rather than the Detroit side, because that way they will avoid paying the higher taxes of the Motor City.

Hamtramck was a contentious plant before it was even built. To make way for its construction, the city knocked down much of the neighborhood known as Poletown, which had been settled by Polish immigrants who came to labor in the auto industry in the 1920s and 1930s. According to the *Detroit Free Press*, "1,300 homes, 140 businesses, six churches and one hospital lay in the path of the proposed plant."[1]

Despite an offer by the city, led by Mayor Coleman Young, to buy homes from those displaced and to help finance new ones, the construction rankled residents.

The protests made it to the national level after GM's longtime nemesis got involved: consumer affairs crusader Ralph Nader. His activists decamped to the area with vigils and legal action to back the local residents fighting eviction. Even the venerable *New York Times* columnist William Safire wrote about the controversy, decrying the destruction of a neighborhood by eminent domain.[2] With the prospect of up to 6,000 jobs for a city that was struggling with 18 percent unemployment, though, the wrecking ball won out.

GM aimed to make the plant a showcase of modern factory automation when it began production in 1985 with a Cadillac Eldorado, installing expensive robotic systems. But Hamtramck didn't quite live up to the hype. The cars coming off the line, like those across GM, were behind many of their rivals in quality. The plant was one of the hotbeds of union activity, and relations with Local 22 of the United Auto Workers (UAW) could be strained.

It was at this plant that Mary Barra finally reached the career goal she had first sketched out with Ken Varisco years earlier while working at the tech center. In 2003, Gary Cowger, who by then had become president of the company's North American operations, named Barra the plant manager.

The role is traditionally a proving ground for future top managers at GM, to test how they did running the heart of the company's business. The thinking was that if you could handle the complexity of running an auto assembly plant the size of a small city, you could handle managing a division of the company. Cowger says it was the toughest job Barra had taken on so far. "We really threw her off the deep end with that one," he says, sounding amused at the recollection.

Since leaving her post in internal communications in 2001, Barra had been working for Cowger as executive director of the company's competitive operations engineering. Cowger, like Barra, an alumnus of General Motors Institute, had adapted the lean manufacturing methods developed by Japanese carmakers to GM's own processes. Barra was tapped to be his ambassador to manufacturing engineering staff about the need to adopt the Global Manufacturing System (GMS), GM's production system—something that was being implemented unevenly.

At Hamtramck, she would no longer be trying to get people to follow someone else's orders. She'd be giving them herself. And she'd have to establish her authority quickly.

Her years working in plants served her well. Larry Zahner, who had taken the senior leadership class with Barra and was her direct boss at the time, was struck by how she walked around the shop floor and knew the names of workers and details about their personal lives, like what their children were doing in the evening, or who might be going to night school to get a degree. At the same time, she was no pushover. "People who gave her lip, she'd come right back and tell them the facts," says Mark Sullivan, another manufacturing executive at the time. "In the plants, you really have to be direct or you're going to be dead meat."

Barra says she concentrated on communications from the start, because the plant had had a lot of leadership turnover. She wrote a weekly article for the plant newsletter, would pass out a daily sheet with production statistics, and would also communicate via closed-caption TV that was beamed to each production team's location. "It was to let them know you really cared about the plant," she says.

Not only was Hamtramck one of the company's largest plants; it was also one of its most complex. In 2003 the plant was building six models from three different marques, and had 3,400 workers on two shifts. Today, when staff has declined to just 1,600, DHAM, as company insiders call it, still produces multiple vehicles, including the Chevrolet Volt electric car, the Chevy Impala, and the Cadillac ELR.[3]

Staff and managers career around the plant's 3.6 million square feet of space in open-topped electric trucks and forklifts, where road signs and wall-mounted mirrors help prevent collisions. On the lines, workers solder steering columns, wire in stereo systems, or supervise the robots that stamp bodies and paint vehicles. If a worker detects a defect or has a problem as the car passes his (or her) station, he pulls a yellow cord and a chime sounds—the automotive equivalent of a ring tone—and numbers light up on the so-called Andon board, an innovation borrowed from the Japanese that tracks the line's production, so everyone can see where the problems are.

Such accoutrements, now standard in the industry, were cutting-edge in 2003. At the time, GM was spending about $1,500 more to build each vehicle than Toyota was, according to a Goldman Sachs analysis cited by *Bloomberg News*.[4] Between the loss-making and the decline in sales following the September 11, 2001, terrorist attacks in the United States, plants were under pressure to reduce costs. Cowger increased the target for budget trims that year to as much as 10 percent, up from an earlier target of 3 to 7 percent. "We've got to adjust on the run," Cowger told *Bloomberg News* at the time. Competition "is getting more intense every day." Meanwhile, credit agencies were lowering their rating on GM debt, which would ultimately decline to junk status in mid-2005.[5]

To help meet Cowger's targets, the company told workers it planned to slow down the production line at the plant, which could have resulted in as many as 600 layoffs, according to the *Detroit Free Press*, which cited a decline in sales of three of the models Hamtramck produced: the Cadillac Seville and DeVille and the Buick LeSabre.[6]

"We had some challenges," Barra concedes. "The plant had been pretty steady-state for several years; then I went in and we had to de-rate the line." That meant slowing down the speed of the production line when it was producing fewer cars. The result was that there might be only 50 one-minute tasks to accomplish per hour rather than 60. So either everybody's job would have to be changed, or there would need to be layoffs.

In the past, the plant manager would have asked each department for a list of workers to be furloughed, says Alicia Boler-Davis, who was manager of the general assembly area at the time. Another rising young female engineer, Boler-Davis oversaw the largest department of the plant, where workers attach most of the car's components to its body.

Barra took a different route. She methodically worked with each department to add content to the line jobs so that they would effectively use the full hour. "That meant that every single job on the line changed," she says. Boler-Davis recalls that previously cars were being built quickly on the line and then "rebuilt" downstream as a second set of workers made adjustments of parts that hadn't been positioned to meet specifications. When Barra slowed the line, workers had time to do the job correctly the first time.

"I learned a lot by watching her approach," Boler-Davis says. "She's humble, which makes people want to work for her. At the same time, she's pushing you to do more."

Barra also got buy-in from the UAW shop chairman at the plant, Frank Moultrie. The fact that she was a woman and a plant manager got a lot of attention at the time, Moultrie says, and also made her easier to deal with than some of her predecessors. "She broke through the glass ceiling," he says. "There was a lot of interest in that."

At first, plant workers were careful to "mind their p's and q's around her," he says, which changed the atmosphere at the plant. "Anytime you have a woman in charge, it decreases the amount of testosterone in the room," he says. "Men have a tendency to want to have a swordfight." Barra was someone he could sit down and talk with.

Barra also had to reorganize the way work was done. In the past, a single shop supervisor might have had 50 or 60 line employees to oversee. It was almost impossible to keep track of everybody, and just keep them on the line. Under Barra, the employees would be broken into teams of five or six, each with a team leader who would report up to a group leader, who be responsible to the supervisor. The structure was inspired by Japanese manufacturing methods that empowered workers.

The team leader would have to make sure that his or her team of half a dozen people met its production quotas. Even if one member needed time off on a certain day and production slipped, the team would have to make it up the next day. The team leader might be focused on a day's output, and would meet with team members regularly and know in detail how each of them was performing. The leader's next boss was a group leader, who would make sure that the teams reporting to him or her met weekly targets; next up was a supervisor, who might be looking at things on a monthly basis.

Zahner says that at first some union members were reluctant to adopt the system and wanted to know why meeting targets was their job. "We do what we're told" and "We have certain work rules we have to follow" were the responses, he says.

"That was a growing pain for all of us," Moultrie says. "We were still a bit skeptical. She helped us understand that this was a global manufacturing system" and that every company in the world was adopting similar methods.

There were pros as well as cons, though. The managers were for the first time encouraged to listen to input from the workers. A manager had to realize that just because an idea came from a union worker instead of himself, it didn't mean his job was in jeopardy. And who better than the person who actually put bolts on the car to suggest better ways of doing that?

Barra employed what Cowger calls "the velvet glove and the iron fist." She'd be warm and friendly, but hold people accountable for their actions. If a shift began at 6:30 A.M., the workers were expected to be at their stations and ready to start at that time. "It was really about getting people to do the jobs that they are paid to do," says Zahner.

There were major challenges to the company coming from outside, in terms of both competition and shifts in the market for autos. Changes were needed if the company was to make money. Poor quality might not necessarily have been the result of workers intentionally goofing off. Working for hours on the repetitive tasks on the assembly line, they may have been distracted by personal problems or other issues. But at the end of the day, they were letting down their team if they didn't show up on time and work to a high standard. That was a message Barra tried to instill.

Quality was a big problem for the plant. "We struggled for a while," she says. "There's not a lot of tolerance for a plant not meeting schedule." Barra called the plant leadership together and told them that quality would be the number-one focus; schedule would come second. "Miraculously, the quality got better, and you know what? The schedule followed," she says. "It was remarkable."

Barra had to take off her velvet glove at times. "There were a couple of people who weren't really team players," she says. "They are no longer with the company."

She also negotiated with the UAW so that workers could rotate into different tasks throughout a shift, something that the union once more resisted at first. The aim, which again was adopted from Japanese carmakers, was that the worker might learn how to do various parts of the car's assembly. That not only gave the company more flexibility in deploying its workers; it also helped reduce some of the repetitive strain injuries common to autoworkers.

And by making multiple models in the plant—as opposed to only one or two as had often been the case in the past—the company would be able to adjust production to what customers were buying. As obvious as that sounds, that hadn't always been the case previously. Factories just made cars and waited for customers to buy them.

Barra still clashed with the union at times. The first year she was at Hamtramck, she told Moultrie that the company was going to save on the electricity cost of putting up the Christmas lights that typically lined the drive up to the plant during the holiday season.

"I said, 'Really?'" Moultrie says. "Is it really that bad?" Barra agreed that the lights would help raise the spirits of workers, especially at a time when they were under continual pressure from management to work differently. He and Barra agreed to split the costs out of their own pockets—maybe $200 or $300 in total.

Barra also negotiated about hours for the workers in the plant. If they had to be cut, she might agree to splitting the workers in groups so that each group could work one week on, one week off. Or in busy times, she wouldn't force workers to work overtime.

Despite her high demands on workers, she was willing to see them as people with families and outside lives, rather than just cogs in a machine. Moultrie remembers one worker who made a "mistake" he won't specify and was about to be fired. As shop chairman, he appealed to Barra: The worker was close to retirement age, and had a stay-at-home wife who would depend on his pension. Barra agreed to reinstate the worker so that he could apply for retirement and get his pension. "She was very approachable," he says.

At Hamtramck, Barra commanded attention of GM's top management as well. Hamtramck wasn't the company's biggest plant or its most profitable. But by virtue of being only a 10-minute drive from the brass at its head office in the Renaissance Center in downtown Detroit, Hamtramck was and still is one of its most visible sites. "Whenever someone came to town and said, 'I'd like to see a plant,' they'd take them to Hamtramck," says Zahner, like Barra, a graduate of General Motors Institute. Years later, one such visitor was President Barack Obama, who stopped by in the summer of 2010, when the automaker had just exited bankruptcy and was still partly owned by the government.

That wasn't the only reason Barra won notice during her time at the plant. Under her leadership it went from a contentious union hotbed with quality problems to one that won plaudits. In 2004, the plant won a Silver Award from J.D. Power & Associates, which ranks North American assembly plants based on production quality. The following year, the plant won a Bronze Award from J.D. Power for the quality of vehicles it produced, behind two other GM plants. Those were the only two years in which the plant ever won. Hamtramck's 2005 model Buick LeSabre, built under Barra's watch, was ranked first for quality among full-sized cars in the ranking, based on a survey of vehicle owners.

Boler-Davis was also impressed by Barra's interest in her career and personal life. "Mary first came to the plant seven or eight months after my son was born," Boler-Davis says. They talked about being moms in a manufacturing environment, about good schools in the area, and about the support needed at home to enable her to advance. Still, it was tough; there was no flextime in her role, Boler-Davis says: "I had to be at work at 5 A.M." Finding reliable child care was paramount (Boler-Davis's mother moved in with her and her husband to help care for her two children).

Barra also applied the lessons she'd been learning to helping others as she was groomed for increasingly powerful roles. She told Boler-Davis, who holds a bachelor's degree in chemical engineering from Northwestern University and a master's from Rensselaer Polytechnic Institute, that she would advance farther and faster if she challenged herself by trying to learn different parts of the manufacturing process. Shortly thereafter, Boler-Davis transferred to GM's Fort Wayne, Indiana, truck plant, where she got experience running the paint shop and the body shop.

"It probably would have been easier for Mary to keep me" at Hamtramck, Boler-Davis says. But Barra didn't let her own short-term interest stand in the way. "She allowed me to leave right before we were ready to launch another vehicle."

In 2007, Bohler-Davis became a plant manager herself, moving to Arlington, Texas. She was one of GM's youngest-ever plant managers at the age of 37 and also the first African American woman to run a GM car-making plant. Later she moved back to Michigan, where she ran the Orion assembly plant and Pontiac stamping plant about 40 miles north of Detroit, while simultaneously working as chief engineer for the launch of the Chevrolet Sonic, a popular subcompact that aimed to show that the company could successfully build small cars in the United States.

As she moved up the ranks, Boler-Davis kept in touch with Barra, using her as a sounding board. "One lesson I learned from her was the importance of expanding my horizons and working in areas outside of manufacturing," she says. In 2012, Boler-Davis became vice president of customer experience, a job Barra encouraged her to take even though she had never worked in customer service. A few months later, she added global quality to her responsibilities.

Today, Boler-Davis works directly for Barra as senior vice president of connected customer experience, one of the top positions at the company.

Notes

1. http://blogs.detroitnews.com/history/2000/01/26/auto-plant-vs-neighborhood-the-poletown-battle/.
2. www.nytimes.com/1981/04/30/opinion/essay-poletown-wrecker-s-ball.html?module=Search&mabReward=relbias%3Ar%2C%7B%221%22%3A%22RI%3A9%22%7D.
3. http://media.gm.com/media/us/en/gm/company_info/facilities/assembly/dham.html.
4. Joe Miller, "General Motors' Wagoner Seeks Savings to Boost Profit (Update1)," *Bloomberg News*, April 15, 2003.
5. Mark Pittman, "General Motors Debt Rating Cut to Junk by Standard & Poor's," *Bloomberg News*, May 5, 2005.
6. Jeffrey McCracken, "GM Will Slow Line and Lay Off 500–600," *Detroit Free Press*, January 20, 2003.

The car that started it all: a Pontiac Firebird, circa 1970. Barra's cousin had a red convertible model that ignited her love for cars.

Photo credit: General Motors

Mary Makela and Barb Gesaman (*left*) were co-editors of their yearbook at Waterford Mott high school, where Mary was one of 10 seniors with a perfect 4.0 grade point average.

Photo credit: Waterford Mott High School yearbook/courtesy Waterford School District

Makela was also voted the girl most likely to succeed in the class of 1980. The caption reads: It's just five more miles to the poorhouse.

Photo credit: Waterford Mott High School yearbook/courtesy Waterford School District

Mary Makela earned a degree in electrical engineering from General Motors Institute, now Kettering University, in Flint, Michigan.

Photo credit: Kettering University Archives, Flint, Michigan

Makela (*front row, third from left*) was a member of Beta Theta Pi, a "little sister" organization affiliated with the fraternity of the same name, where she met her future husband, Tony Barra.

General Motors Institute's main academic building, circa 1980. The building is still in use today for classroom and laboratory space.

The Fiero plant in Pontiac, Michigan, where Barra worked while a coop student and after graduating from General Motors Institute, was one of the first plants to adopt Japanese manufacturing methods.

Photo credit: General Motors

A 1984 Fiero. The car was only built for a few years in the mid–1980s, but it continues to have a cult following today.

Photo credit: General Motors

Photo credit: Susan Ragan/Bloomberg News

Photo credit: Susan Ragan/Bloomberg News

Two views of Stanford University, where Mary Barra earned her MBA at the Graduate School of Business in 1990. In 2014, Barra hired Stanford to create an executive training program for General Motors.

Barra was hired in 1997 as executive assistant to CEO Jack Smith, left, and vice chairman Harry Pearce, shown here about 1995.

Photo credit: General Motors

Photo credit: Laura Colby

Photo credit: Naftali Raz

General Motors moved its headquarters into the Renaissance Center on the Detroit River from a downtown building at about the same time.

Photo credit: General Motors

Photo credit: General Motors

Barra became the manager of the Hamtramck auto assembly plant, which sprawls over both the city of Detroit and the town of Hamtramck, in 2003. Under her leadership, the plant improved quality and won several awards.

Photo credit: Laura Colby

Photo credit: Laura Colby

Photo credit: Jeffrey Sauger/Bloomberg News

Barra was based several times in her career at the General Motors Technical Center in Warren, Michigan, outside Detroit. The modernist campus, whose silver dome is used to display new car models, was designed in 1949 by Eero Saarinen, like Barra of Finnish heritage. The center, which was designated a National Historic Landmark in 2000, was a location for the "Transformers" films, which feature characters based on GM cars.

Rick Wagoner, then-CEO, testified before the House Financial Service Committee in December 2008 about why the company needed government funds. Saturday Night Live later lampooned him, as they would with Barra after her testimony on the ignition switch six years later.

Photo credit: Jim Lo Scalzo/Bloomberg News

When Ed Whitacre became CEO following the company's bankruptcy in 2009, he wrote in his autobiography, "The "new" GM was just like the old GM, except it was smaller and had $50 billion in taxpayer money."

Photo credit: Jeff Kowalsky/Bloomberg News

Bob Lutz, the quintessential "car guy" and a Barra predecessor in global product development, says GM's current car models show Barra was able to fend off any attempts by the finance side to cheapen them.

Photo credit: Jeff Kowalsky/Bloomberg News

CEO Dan Akerson promoted Barra to head of product development and later chose her as his successor when he stepped down in December of 2013.

Photo credit: Andrew Harrer/Bloomberg

Photo credit: Steve Fecht for General Motors

Photo credit: Lee Anderson for Chevrolet

Barra after being named Vice President in charge of global product development in 2011, and while in that role as she introduced a Chevy Colorado pickup.

Barra with Mark Reuss, another GM lifer who succeeded her as head of global product development, at the North American International Auto Show in Detroit in January 2014, shortly before she took over as CEO.

Photo credit: Andrew Harrer/Bloomberg

Dan Ammann, who joined General Motors following its bankruptcy from Morgan Stanley, is now Barra's second in command as the company president.

Photo credit: Scott Eells/Bloomberg

Less than three months into her CEO job, Barra was grilled by a Senate subcommittee in April 2014 about why the company had failed to recall cars with a faulty ignition switch for more than a decade.

Photo credit: Andrew Harrer/Bloomberg

One of the recalled models in which several people died was the Chevrolet Cobalt, which is no longer made, shown here at a dealership in 2010.

Photo credit: Jeff Kowalsky/Bloomberg News

Senator Barbara Boxer scolded Barra during the hearings in April for her inability to answer detailed questions about the ignition switch, saying she was disappointed "woman to woman."

Photo credit: Andrew Harrer/Bloomberg

Senator Claire McCaskill softened her tone during Barra's second testimony in July, praising her for her decisive response. "I think you've handled this with courage and conviction," she told Barra.

Photo credit: Andrew Harrer/Bloomberg

Photo credit: Steve Fecht for General Motors

Photo credit: John F. Martin for General Motors

Barra held a town hall meeting for employees worldwide to disclose the devastating results of the Valukas report into the faulty ignition switch. "I don't want to forget what happened because I never want this to happen again."

Photo credit: Steve Fecht for General Motors

Photo credit: Michael Nagle/Bloomberg

While the switch fiasco took much of her time, Barra still made some unrelated public appearances as CEO in 2014. In May, she gave the commencement address at the University of Michigan in Ann Arbor. In November, Barra was a panelist at the Clinton Global Initiative with, from left, Chelsea Clinton, Alibaba's Jack Ma, Nigerian Finance Minister Ngozi Okonjo-Iweala, and Darren Walker, president of the Ford Foundation.

Barra met her husband, Tony, in college and says he has been very supportive of her career.

Photo credit: Steve Fecht for General Motors

Chapter 9

Chevy Avalanche:
The Road to Ruin

M ary Barra's management at Hamtramck may have helped set the plant on the right path, but it was just one plant of many at the automaker that were facing similar quality problems. In 2004, she was called back to the trenches of manufacturing, again working for Cowger.

General Motors at this time was, in Barra's words, "a cost culture." Under CEO Rick Wagoner, who had taken on the chairman role as well in 2003, when Jack Smith retired, GM was losing money on almost every car it sold—racking up a total of some $82 billion in annual losses by the time the company filed for bankruptcy protection in 2009.[1] The statistic was even more stunning when you considered that Wagoner, who holds a degree in economics from Duke University as well as an MBA, had risen through the financial side of the company and had served as chief financial officer. If he couldn't make the numbers add up, who could?

To be fair, there was an elephant in the room. The company was carrying huge, crippling costs of providing benefits—including a health care package with virtually no co-pay—to thousands of retirees and their families, agreed on in better times. The burden would eventually help push the company over the brink.

Focusing on numbers alone wouldn't help GM, whose products continued to leave consumers unenthused. "There's got to be arguing between the people who are fighting for product excellence and customer satisfaction on the one hand and the people who want to save money on the other," says Bob Lutz, who was now the company's vice chairman responsible for global product development. He complains that his efforts to improve quality or styling of cars during the period were often blocked because it would mean failing to meet cost metrics.

Barra was now executive director of manufacturing engineering, the side of the business that figures out how cars will be made, by what processes and machines, and in which plants. Following on the lean manufacturing methods she had helped Cowger implement with the GM Production System earlier in the decade, she instituted what were called lean reviews. Managers would look at all the different steps of car manufacturing, such as stamping, dies, welding tools, paint, and general assembly. She'd carefully analyze the amount of money needed for each of those departments to build a vehicle, then benchmark it against the global leader in that field in terms of quality and cost, and try to match or exceed that.

As a manufacturing engineer, Barra's job could at times put her at loggerheads with the engineers who were developing new cars. Often, the cars were designed and then the designs were handed over to manufacturing to figure out how to make them—only to discover that it would be technically impossible or prohibitively expensive. They'd have to scrap the design. "It was a big manufacturing silo: 'Stay away—don't touch my stuff!'" says Mark Reuss, an engineer on the product side, who had met Barra for the first time while she ran Hamtramck and developed respect for her. "Here's a woman in a pretty big place of power, who's around my age, so I thought it was pretty cool," he says.

Barra decided that her staff should attend Reuss's team meetings, and vice versa. Product people had "lots of resistance to someone from manufacturing sitting in on their meetings," he says. Barra also took flak from her bosses, who didn't like having manufacturing people interfacing so closely with the product team. She set up a monthly engineering meeting where both sides could air their disagreements and solve them. "It was pretty big," Reuss says.

Barra says she was simply putting her communications skills to work. "When you put two groups of engineers together and they truly understand each other's problems, they're going to solve them," she says.

Cowger, impressed, increased her responsibilities, eventually putting her in charge of all manufacturing engineering, where she was tasked with coming up with more efficient ways of building cars to help boost the bottom line. By 2008, she was in charge of engineering not only in North America but everywhere in the world and had finally earned the title her boss back in the 1990s, Varisco, had predicted she'd one day achieve: vice president. She began traveling frequently to the European plants of Adam Opel AG, GM's Germany-based subsidiary, and those of GM's joint ventures in China, which was soon to become the world's largest auto market, as well as its other international units.

By that time, the global economic hurricane that had been howling through financial markets since the collapse of Lehman Brothers Holdings had hit the auto business hard. Consumer credit dried up, and even those who didn't need credit held back from buying cars as storied Wall Street names either went under, merged, or trekked to Washington with their hats in hand.

General Motors was burning through its cash so quickly that without more borrowing, the company would be unable to pay its creditors by the end of the year. But the same credit crunch that had dampened consumer spending meant that even a giant household name like GM couldn't get a loan. It didn't help that the company's debt had been trading as junk since 2005.[2] The other Detroit automakers weren't much better off.

The government had already extended emergency backing to Wall Street firms to stave off a global financial collapse. In November, it was the Big Three's turn to plead for government help. GM had laid off thousands of workers and closed plants, but it was still going to be broke by the end of the year unless it got financing, CEO Wagoner told a skeptical Congress. (He and the other U.S. auto chiefs were widely derided in the press afterward for taking a private jet to Washington at a time when their companies, and the country, were struggling.)

After a second hearing in December, President George W. Bush, a lame duck, issued an executive order giving GM and Chrysler $17.4 billion of funds on the condition that by February the company come up with a plan to return to health. Wagoner, Chrysler's Robert Nardelli, and Ford's Alan Mullaly were lampooned on television's *Saturday Night Live* comedy show, which depicted the leaders as having driven to Washington from Detroit in vehicles that had major quality problems. Wagoner personally took the worst skewering, with his character shown as presenting financial charts that demonstrated the company would be back for more government aid within six months, and again every six months after that.

Though it was meant as satire, that aspect of the sketch wasn't too far from the truth. By late January, shortly after President Barack Obama took office, it was clear that the line of credit wasn't enough.

In late December, the company had presented a plan to Congress to back up its request for a government handout. John F. Smith (no relation to the former chairman/CEO), who was in charge of global planning at the time, got together with a group of top managers from product design, finance, and manufacturing to help their company fight for its life. Among them was Barra, representing manufacturing engineering. Hunkered down in a conference room at the Renaissance Center, a few floors below Wagoner's executive suite, the group met for what seemed like days on end, recalls Smith. "We were spinning out drafts daily," he recalls. Barra and her team helped draft those reports.

As the company desperately tried to stave off bankruptcy, on several occasions Wagoner would ask Smith and his group to come up with cuts of $1.5 billion or $2 billion out of the capital budget. "These were difficult, time-critical meetings," Smith says. Barra, no more happy than anyone else about the cuts, nonetheless understood the gravity of the task and was able to gather up financials to support any decision. "She has a way of remaining calm and collected," Smith says.

The bankruptcy was like a huge asset sale. "Every piece of equipment in every one of our plants plus our facilities were under manufacturing engineering," says Barra. "I had the engineering and I had the facilities group, so a huge portion of the assets of the company that we had to make decisions on were my responsibility." Barra had to help decide which plants were going to close, and then carry out those closures. "We had to make very difficult decisions," she said.

On February 17, the GM task force presented a plan to return to profitability within 24 months.

President Obama's representatives rejected it. It wasn't drastic enough—too incremental, they said. The President gave the company a June 1 deadline for coming up with a more substantial restructuring plan, and extended credit to keep the company afloat. In the meantime, under pressure from the government, Wagoner resigned and was replaced by Fritz Henderson, a GM veteran who, like Wagoner, had come up through the financial side of the company.

Finally, on June 1, 2009, the company filed for protection from its creditors under Chapter 11 of the U.S. Bankruptcy Code in a New York court. GM had assets of $82.3 billion and liabilities of $172.8 billion, according to the filing.[3] Only months into his first term, President Obama took a policy gamble and agreed to inject $30 billion more into the company, in addition to some $20 billion in loans made previously.

In return, the U.S. Treasury got a 60 percent stake in what would be dubbed the "new GM." Other shareholders included an employee health care fund with 17.5 percent, the Canadian government with 12 percent, and bondholders with the remainder.[4]

By agreeing to take stakes in the company, the governments of the United States and Canada saved not only thousands of jobs for GM workers, but also hundreds of thousands of other jobs in the web of suppliers, dealers, and companies that indirectly relied on GM and its employees as customers. With the global economy in a slump, GM was considered "too big to fail." That decision remains controversial to this day, with detractors pointing out that the government ultimately lost $11 billion on the bailout.

As part of the agreement, GM agreed to drop four of its eight North American brands. It would sell Hummer and Saab, and would quit making Saturns, once the company's standard-bearer of a new model of management-labor relations.

Under the plan GM submitted, one Pontiac model would have survived as a "youthful, sporty niche brand"—a faint echo of the long-ago slogan "Pontiac builds excitement" when the company was selling the

took early retirement at age 63. Barra's friend and longtime booster in human resources, Cheri Alexander, had retired in 2008, prior to the bankruptcy, to teach at the University of Michigan. Maureen Kempston Darkes, one of the highest-ranking women at the company, who at the time headed the company's operations in Europe, Africa, and the Middle East, ended her decades-long career with GM at the age of 60 and returned to practicing law. Kempston Darkes, who'd had her eye on Barra as an up-and-comer ever since she worked in the CEO's office and helped set up the women's groups, says she advised Barra to stick with the company.

Even so, Barra thought about quitting. "There was a time during the bankruptcy when I went, 'Whoa,' and did some soul-searching," she says. Ultimately, she chose to stay. "I decided I wanted to be part of the team that turned GM around."

Like Reuss, Barra had taken on a new role after the bankruptcy—Henderson had tapped her to be head of human resources. It seemed like a poisoned chalice in more ways than one. First, Barra would have to preside over personnel at a time when many were leaving—not always voluntarily. And she'd have to recruit new, talented people to replace them at a time when the company was on its knees and restricted by the government as to what it could pay. In addition, the role was what's referred to in corporate-speak as a "staff" job—one that was far from making cars and that wouldn't use her engineering skills. Such roles are often reserved for women, and despite being at the top of the executive ranks, they generally are dead ends that don't lead to the CEO position.[1]

Emerging from bankruptcy protection just a month after the June 8, 2009, filing was what would be called the "new GM." To say that its CEO, Henderson, had inherited a tough job is a drastic understatement. He had to answer to a newly activist board of directors, many members of which had been installed by the company's government overseer, Steve Rattner, who became known as the Car Czar. Among them were three from the world of private equity: Daniel Akerson, David Bonderman, and Stephen Girsky. All were used to scrutinizing the financial details of deals and asked tougher questions in the boardroom than the company's management was used to.[2] Heading this newly active board was the former chief executive of AT&T, Edward Whitacre Jr., a Texas native with no background in the auto industry. CEO Henderson was yet another longtime GM employee, who had run the company's European and Asian operations, among other jobs. Some observers wondered whether someone with that background could help create a "new GM" from the ashes of the old one.

GM also had to answer to its new largest shareholder: the U.S. Treasury. That meant more than just questioning management decisions in the boardroom. As a condition of the bailout agreement that had wags referring to the company as Government Motors, Obama's so-called Car Czar had authority to approve the pay packages for the top 25 most highly compensated executives. Pay for the next 75 would also be subject to government-imposed guidelines.

"It was an extraordinary time," recalls Kenneth Feinberg, the attorney who was tapped by the Obama administration to represent the Treasury in setting the pay. Boston native Feinberg, a specialist in mediation, had developed a reputation for fairness as the man in charge of compensating victims of disasters such as the September 11, 2001, terrorist attacks. He was charged with setting compensation for executives of all the companies that received government aid through the Troubled Asset Relief Program (TARP). That included Citigroup, American International Group (AIG), and Chrysler, not just General Motors. It was a long way from the days when corporate and finance chieftains could command salaries well into the seven or even eight figures.

Even Feinberg's title reflected the humiliation of a once-proud company: He was called the Special Master on Executive Compensation. It was time, Feinberg says, for "populist revenge." His job was to balance the desire of the general public and some members of Congress to extract a pound of flesh from the GM brass with an effort at fairness to individuals.

Sitting across the table from the Special Master, pleading for fairness for GM's top brass was Mary Barra.

The Treasury had set a recommended cap on cash pay of $500,000 a year—a fraction of what some of the top executives had been making previously. Special arguments would have to be made to go above that amount. Barra proposed ways of compensating the executives with stock, bonuses, and delayed compensation tied to the company's performance. There could be no guaranteed cash bonuses, no tax abatements, and no perks valued at more than $25,000—about the price of a Chevy

Malibu sedan. The latter wasn't a problem for GM executives, Feinberg said, because most of the perks had been shed earlier as GM desperately, but unsuccessfully, tried to stave off bankruptcy. By the time Feinberg was blue-lining the proposed pay packages, Wagoner's trek via the company jet to Washington a year earlier was only an embarrassing memory. The company had shed its half dozen executive jets, according to Greg Lau, then the head of compensation. Feinberg did allow the executives to charter planes at times, he says.

Barra had prepared dossiers on each executive. "She came loaded for bear," Feinberg says of their negotiations. She knew in great detail what each one personally did and what his or her value to the company was. "She represented the executives and they had trust in her to do what was best," Lau says.

Despite the obvious tension involved in having to slash your bosses'—and your own—pay, the meetings were not adversarial, Feinberg says. "She was extraordinarily bright, very engaging, and very flexible," he says. The flexibility was most evident when it came to determining what proportion of pay would be in stock rather than cash, and whether it would be deferred.

Still, Barra didn't get all she asked for. In Feinberg's final report to the Treasury in 2010, he agreed to allow only eight of the top executives to exceed the $500,000 pay cap, rather than the 16 the GM side sought. Only two employees got a raise in salary, while five had their pay frozen and the remainder of the 25 had their pay cut. The top 25 executives—who presumably included Barra, now that she was one of the top corporate officers as head of HR—still got substantial stock awards, payable over three years, but were forbidden to participate in any hedging or derivatives bets on the GM stock that might let them make money if the company didn't do well. GM was also banned from doling out any "gross up" payments that would mitigate their income tax bills.

Barra and Feinberg developed a mutual respect that led Barra to call on him five years later to figure out how GM should compensate victims of a defective ignition switch.

At first, Barra seemed like an odd choice for HR, given her training as an engineer. But her previous stint in corporate communications helped. Lau recalls that he first crossed paths with her then, and that she knew well how to communicate salary and benefits to both workers and executives. And she had helped improve morale at the company's U.S. plants following a devastating strike. If ever there was a time when the company needed someone who knew how to boost morale, it was during the bankruptcy. When Katy Barclay, the previous head of HR, retired during the bankruptcy, Barra was at the top of the succession list.

The role held a lot of power in shaping the company's future management. Thousands of people were leaving the company. Barra's job was to maintain morale among the most promising ones—the high achievers—so that they wouldn't bolt at a time when they could get bigger salaries elsewhere.

Not all of the departures were voluntary. The board, impatient with the pace of change under Henderson, ousted him in December 2009, less than a year after he had taken charge. Whitacre took on the CEO job himself. He recalls meeting Barra for the first time just after he gave Henderson the news that the board had decided to let him go. Barra, perhaps mindful of the limits the Treasury was placing on CEO pay, asked him how he could take over so quickly when he wasn't even on the payroll. Whitacre says he told her that he would work without pay for a month while they ironed that out. At that point he hadn't even asked the board what his compensation would be.

"We were both new at our jobs," Whitacre recalls in his mild drawl. "It was chaotic."

Barra became a fixture at Whitacre's weekly management meetings, all held in the boardroom atop the Renaissance Center, with its sweeping vistas of the Detroit River and the city's decaying downtown. Their offices were a stone's throw apart, and the pair talked frequently about personnel as Whitacre sought to create a management team for the new GM. "I sought her opinion about the abilities of different people," he says. "We were trying to change the entire management." He relied on Barra for advice about the skills of those who remained.

So did Reuss, who had been named North American president three months after the bankruptcy. "It was carnage," he says. "We had to bring the company public, we had to put a new team together in sales and marketing, and we had to clean house in terms of the people who were doing that job here." Barra sat in on Reuss's team meetings and went to visit job candidates with him. "It was massive," he says. "We had to go convince people this was going to be a new company and a new place."

Whitacre's blunt style helped drive home the message that this wasn't the old GM. As he recounts it in his 2013 book, *American Turnaround*,[3] top management at GM when he arrived in Detroit as chairman seemed to regard the bankruptcy as if it had just been "a messy misunderstanding." "There was little urgency that I could detect; no larger sense of purpose," he wrote. "The 'new' GM was just like the old GM, except it was smaller and had $50 billion in taxpayer money."

Whitacre didn't hide his feelings, and his meetings were at times uncomfortable, with even the highest-level executives silently shifting in their chairs. One person who was willing to challenge him was Barra. "She's no shrinking violet," Whitacre says. "When she disagreed with me, she'd tell me." Rather than be irritated, he says, "I loved it."

In his book he recalls one incident when he decided to hire a former colleague, John Montford, to head the company's office in Washington, D.C. Under government ownership, the lobbying role managing GM's relationships in Washington would be key. Whitacre called Barra and ordered her to get Montford on the payroll the next day. At first, she blanched, noting that big companies usually take 30 days to process a new hire. Then she made it happen, he writes.

By the time Whitacre's tenure ended, much of the top layer of GM's management had been replaced, as well as a good portion of the next tier. Some longtime executives were fired. Others found their responsibilities drastically reduced. Bob Lutz, the car industry design legend who had most recently been the company's vice chairman and had been favored by Henderson, was presumed by some to be in line for the top job. Instead, he was assigned to be an adviser to Whitacre without any direct reports. "I'm fine with the role," Lutz, then 78, told Jeff Green of *Bloomberg News* at the time, "because by his own admission, Ed really doesn't know the mechanics of the business."[4] Lutz continued to consult for company.

Whitacre elevated a younger generation of managers. He especially favored Reuss, then 46, an archtypical "car guy" who is a licensed Grand-Am Road Racing driver. While moving up the product ranks, Reuss had overseen both the wildly successful revival of the Chevrolet Camaro and the notorious flop of the Pontiac Aztek sport-utility vehicle.[5]

Stephen Girsky, 47, a former Morgan Stanley auto analyst, had joined the board as the representative of the UAW. Whitacre brought him on as an adviser and later as vice chairman in early 2010. He also took on responsibility for GM's Opel AG European operations, which the company considered selling during its exit from bankruptcy.

Dan Ammann, the Morgan Stanley banker who had worked on the company's bankruptcy, joined GM full-time in early 2010 as Treasurer and later became CFO. He wasn't yet 40. A couple of years later, all three men would emerge as Barra's rivals for the role of CEO.

At less rarefied levels, Barra had a huge amount of work to do as well. She made use of the bankruptcy filing to try to get employees, from union workers in the plants to salaried office workers, to accept that the company needed to adopt a more entrepreneurial, less bureaucratic way of doing things. Her "hearts and minds" campaign had echoes of the work she'd done a decade earlier while at internal communications.

Lau, who retired from GM in 2012 after a 40-year career, recalls that on Barra's first day on the job in HR, she brought everybody a gift. "It was something you got at Staples, a gadget with a big red button. When you pushed the button, it said, 'That was easy.' The idea was to get us used to the idea that you could make a decision quickly," Lau says.

"We very much wanted to drive a new culture, and to make sure that we were really engaging people and empowering them," Barra recalled in an interview at *Fortune* magazine's 2013 summit on the World's Most Powerful Women.[6] "As difficult as it was to go through the bankruptcy, one of the positive things was you had the emotion and the attention of everybody.... So it was a rare opportunity."

To deliver the message, Barra went on the road, visiting the company's locations across the country. She'd hold brown bag lunches at plants and offices to answer employee questions. She also had a series of more formal meetings with invited representatives from different sections of the company—so-called diagonal slices. With more than a dozen plants closing and thousands of workers laid off, she needed to underline the message that the company wanted those who remained to do their jobs well and to be accountable for the results.

One of the most iconic things Barra did to get the message across that times were changing was to relax the company's dress code. It ran to about 10 pages when she joined HR, including descriptions of proper attire for everyone from assembly line workers to office staff to executives. "It was probably the most interesting change and the biggest learning that I had into a culture," Barra said at the *Fortune* women's forum. She whittled the code down into two words. "We said, 'Dress appropriately.' That was it."

Rather than liberating employees, the change left some of them terrified. Barra said she'd have managers e-mailing or calling her and asking for written details of the policy.

"So I'd take them through, and say, 'What do you do?' And they'd say, 'I manage 20 people and a $10 million budget.' And I'd say, 'I can trust you to manage 20 people and $10 million but I can't trust you to dress appropriately, to figure that out?'"

One former GM executive recalls how articulated the company's management hierarchy was prior to bankruptcy, with labeled steps much like those found in the government service. The system went back at least as far as 1972, when Marguerite Novelli was promoted to be GM's assistant corporate secretary, a job that brought her a private office decorated with a plush French blue carpet, but no bonus.[7] For instance, a manager would have to be at level eight to get a company car; only those at executive level would be eligible for a bonus; and so on.

Decades later, the same hierarchy would stymie certain aspects of the business. Top executives all got BlackBerry devices when they became an important tool. But the BlackBerries and company cell phones were forbidden to employees below a certain level, even when there was a strong business case for them to have one. For instance, a junior public relations official who had to field questions from reporters around the clock might be refused a cell phone.

Under Barra, those things started to ease up. "We found that sometimes people hid behind the rules and didn't like them but didn't necessarily step up," Barra said at the *Fortune* conference. "It became a window into the change we needed to make." Today, a visitor to the Renaissance Center might see any number of GM staffers without neckties or wearing jeans to the office. On many of the Fridays when she is in town, that would include Barra.

Notes

1. Jeff Green, "Women in Great Jobs Still in Wrong Jobs," *Bloomberg News*, August 22, 2014.

2. David Welch and Jeff Green, "Bonderman Using Socratic Method in GM Boardroom Raises Hackles," *Bloomberg News*, December 11, 2009.
3. Ed Whitacre with Leslie Cauley, *American Turnaround: Reinventing AT&T and GM and the Way We Do Business in the USA* (New York: Business Plus/Hachette, 2013), Chapter 1.
4. Jeff Green, "GM's Lutz Extends Stay, Enforces Whitacre's Monday-Meeting Plan," *Bloomberg News*, December 14, 2009.
5. David Welch and Katie Merx, "Whitacre Turns to Aztek Manager to Undo GM Mistakes (Update1)," *Bloomberg News*, December 15, 2009.
6. http://fortune.com/2013/10/16/gms-mary-barra-to-staff-no-more-crappy-cars/.
7. Suzy Farbman, "Auto Women," *Detroit News Sunday Magazine*, May 14, 1972, 20.

Chapter 11

Chevy Cruze: "No More Crappy Cars"

E dward Whitacre's leadership was jarring for some at the company. He wanted to move fast, had little patience for long PowerPoint presentations, and left the 39th-floor CEO suite to drop in unannounced at plants and offices throughout the company—all departures from the norm for the company's top echelons. His cut-to-the-chase style was one element that helped bring the company back to profitability quickly. (The hiving off of billions of dollars of debts, the government cash infusion, and streamlining the product line were some obvious others.) By the end of 2009, the new GM was ready to head back to the stock exchange and sell its shares to the public. The company's board thought that whoever led that process should stay with the company for a while. Whitacre wasn't willing to commit to staying long, so another board member, Dan Akerson, stepped into the role.

He was the fourth CEO of General Motors in 18 months.

Like Whitacre, Akerson had no background in the auto industry. He came to GM from the Washington-based Carlyle Group, a private equity firm known for buying downtrodden or financially troubled companies, revamping them, and then selling them. Carlyle is also known for its ties to governments around the world, experience that would be useful in dealing with officials at the company's largest shareholder: the U.S. government. Akerson had operating experience running a number of companies, including one that had been in bankruptcy.

None of that had prepared him for what he found at GM, though. As a board member he was said to be critical of the company's products[1] and of its management.

At least, most of its management. One person in particular caught his attention at the executive committee meetings that Whitacre had convened every week and that Akerson continued. As the top officers of the company discussed future strategy, Mary Barra displayed far more expertise on the running of the company than could be expected from a human resources (HR) leader.

Akerson was surprised to find Barra in such a role. Human resources is sometimes dismissively referred to as a "pink ghetto"—a sort of dead end where women hold the top roles without hope of going higher or gaining real operating power but whose numbers help corporations show that they have a certain percentage of women in top roles. More than half of the women in executive roles at Standard & Poor's 500 companies are in such staff roles.

It was "the worst application of talent I've ever seen in my life," Akerson later said.[2] "I was sitting there going, 'Why the hell were you in HR?'"

Increasingly, he relied on her insights into the company's culture, which he was trying hard to change. In February 2011, he stunned long-time GMers when he named Barra senior vice president of global product development—essentially putting her in charge of the design, manufacturing, and marketing of all of GM's cars. Barra displaced the company's vice chairman, Tom Stephens, another GM lifer whom Akerson named to a new role as chief technology officer. Stephens, then 63, retired a year later.

"That was very huge chunk of the company," says John Smith, who had worked with Barra in manufacturing before the bankruptcy. "That's where you put the resources and where you get the returns." As head of global product development, Barra ultimately was in charge of some 35,000 people building 100 different cars in 130 countries.

Barra's friend Grace Leiblein had been running GM's operations in Mexico, and then in Brazil during the pre-bankruptcy years. She and Barra kept in touch, with Barra offering career advice and even helping Leiblein prepare a presentation for a board of directors meeting, which she'd never attended before. When Leiblein returned to Detroit in 2012 to head global purchasing, she watched how Akerson interacted with Barra at the weekly executive meetings and was struck by how close they had become. "If there was something that needed to be done, it was either Mary who raised her hand—'I can pull that together'—and took the assignment, or Dan gave her the assignment," Leiblein says.

Suddenly she saw that friend in a different light. Barra was not only a "high-potential" executive, but she was fulfilling that potential and was within striking distance of the very top. "My thought process was, 'Yup, she's on that,'" Leiblein says.

The new position rocketed Barra from corporate cog to public figure, at least to those in the auto industry. It was the highest position any woman had achieved in that field. Barra was dubbed "a woman to watch" in *Crain's Detroit Business*, *Automotive News*, and *Advertising Age* because of the dollars GM spends on marketing its new vehicles. She made *Fortune*'s most powerful women list.

She didn't spend time basking in the limelight, though. In her first year, she did some serious streamlining of the bureaucracy. When she came in, each car model had three engineering executives in charge of it; she reduced that to one. The idea was to stop people from being able to blame others for any failings that occurred: One person would be in charge, and accountable for the results.

The company had been losing about $1 billion a year because of mid-development changes or delays in producing vehicles. As recounted by *Fortune*'s Alex Taylor in 2012: "I was confident all the churn was coming from marketing," Barra told an employee group. "I would have bet a paycheck on it. So we did an audit and all the changes came from [engineering]. So we faced the ugly truth."[3] She repeatedly vowed that once decisions on a car were made, they would go forward and stay on schedule.

There were some exceptions, though. Bob Lutz, who preceded Barra as head of product development and continued with the company for several years as a consultant, recalls viewing a model of the next-generation Chevy Cruze in 2012 with Barra, Mark Reuss, and others. The Cruze, introduced for the 2009 model year while Lutz was in charge, is one of GM's most successful small cars, usually ranking among the top sellers in the category. "I said, 'Guys, you can't be serious. This is ugly,'" Lutz says of the redesigned model. "She never said anything. Just dead silence."

She did act, though: The redesign of the car was delayed, with just slight updates introduced in the 2014 and 2015 model years. "It wasn't bad; people liked it," says Reuss, who was head of sales at the time, adding that fixing a car is "expensive and painful." But ultimately, he and Barra decided to do it. "We sat and looked at each other and said, 'I don't want to spend another cycle of my life with another car that could have been better,'" he says. "Good enough isn't enough." Now, Barra has set a goal of trying to get it right the first time. "That's the next level of excellence here," Reuss says.

As for Lutz, there was action in his direction as well. "Shortly after blasting the hell out of [the Cruze], I was politely advised that my consulting contract would end at the end of the calendar year," he says.

Lutz says Barra showed a lot of backbone as head of product development. He recalls his own battles with the finance team over adding trim or other features that would make cars look better and appeal more to customers, but increase costs by several hundred dollars per vehicle. He says she protected the cars that were developed under his leadership but came out after his departure, such as the Cadillac ATS and CTS. "There would have been enough time to ruin them by 'value engineering,' which is a euphemism for taking all the good stuff out," he says. "I think she just absolutely resisted."

Barra would constantly challenge her design and engineering teams to try harder to solve any disagreements they had, says Renee Stephens, who worked in quality control at GM for 28 years until 2014 and attended many meetings with Barra, Reuss, and design chief Ed Welburn where decisions were made about new car models. "She always wanted to challenge the team to find a better way to do things so that we don't compromise the customer. She'd say, 'Can't we do this a different way?'" Stephens says. For instance, the design team might want a rounded vent on a car for esthetic reasons, but every time it would open it would blow onto the driver, whose hands would freeze. "Cost was always a consideration," Stephens says, "but she would spend money where the customer would notice."

Unlike Lutz, who is famed for being frank and opinionated to the point of alienating some of the people he refers to as "bean coun-ters," Barra was able to build bridges with them. Dan Ammann, a New Zealand native who while at Morgan Stanley had advised the automaker during its prebankruptcy days, had joined GM afterward as treasurer and then was promoted to chief financial officer (CFO). He sat in on Barra's product team meetings and tried to explain the financial side of the busi-ness to them, giving them simplified tools to make a quick cost-benefit analysis. "I wouldn't say it was the stereotypical CFO being Dr. No," he says. People who wanted more money for a specific feature or car had the data in front of them to know whether they were on budget. "It was all very transparent," he says. "If something was a close call, we'd get together and talk about it."

She also kept her good relationship with Reuss, which had strength-ened while the two battled through the bankruptcy. "She had helped me so much when she was in HR," he says. "I had been in product devel-opment a lot, and she had not. So while she had helped me with the sales and marketing and the HR, I was like 'How can I help you? I'm here.'" Reuss was promoted to president of North America, and today holds Barra's former job, one of the most powerful in the company.

As CEO, Barra is flanked by Reuss and Ammann at most public appearances, and she defers to them on their specific areas of expertise. Years earlier she had told Mary Sipes, who succeeded her as an aide to Smith and Pearce, about the importance of building relationships as you rise through the corporation. "You can't wait until you need it to create a relationship, because then it will be too late," Sipes recalls her saying.

Barra kept the pressure on her subordinates, including Sipes, who was now head of global product planning, a job that, among other things, helps figure out what features will be on future cars and when they can be adopted. Sipes was working on a new technology that needed to be rolled out on future cars and her team proposed putting the technology into two car models the first year, then more models the second year.

Barra pushed her to double that pace. "She asked, 'Do we need to be that measured?'" Sipes says. "It sounded like it was too comfortable a pace." Since the technology was something that was customer-facing—it would be noticed by the average driver—Barra wanted more of it, and faster. "We had never been given a specific target before," Sipes says. Her team complied.

Barra herself had whittled the focus of her job down to a four-word slogan: "No more crappy cars." In the past, GM would produce cars that were contenders in market segments, not killers. But as Reuss says, good enough was no longer enough.

She passed the message through the ranks. Charlie Gandy-Thompson, an electronics engineer who works in the Warren tech center, says that before Barra took over, "you'd see the executives walking in the hallway" once in a while. Barra held regular meetings with staff to explain what was going on at the company and to take questions. "That's what I liked about her: She made sure communications were always flowing," Gandy-Thompson says. "You wouldn't feel so isolated."

Under Barra, several new cars came out that won strong reviews. While she ran product development, Chevrolet introduced an Impala that *U.S. News & World Report* ranked as the No. 1 affordable large car, while the Chevrolet Corvette was ranked the No. 1 luxury sports car.[4] The ranking is based on third-party reviews. In 2014, GM cars came out on top in six categories of quality in the annual survey by J.D. Power & Associates—all cars that had been designed and built under Barra. The annual survey by Westlake Village, California–based J.D. Power tracks the number of consumer complaints per 100 vehicles in the first 90 days of new vehicle ownership.

"These are products as a result of Mary Barra at the helm," says Lutz. "Maybe she isn't driving the excellence, but she is listening to the people who are driving the excellence and not letting the finance people set damaging and unrealistic goals in terms of what the car can cost. That'll work just as well."

To Akerson, Barra was working very well indeed. By May 2012, he was interviewed by the *Wall Street Journal* about GM's efforts to promote women, and called Barra "one of the most gifted executives I've ever met."[5] He added that she was in the running to be his successor, but not the only candidate.

One of the others was CFO Ammann. "It was clear from the moment Dan Akerson took over that he wasn't going to be a 10-year CEO," Ammann says. "With the passage of time it became clear what the general composition of the next generation of leadership of the company was going to be," though the specific roles weren't yet determined. Akerson had started a process to select his successor, narrowing it down to several finalists over a series of months. He even called in executive coaches to work with each of them.[6]

In 2013, Barra, Ammann, and Reuss had emerged as the top three, Ammann says. "Mary and I took the initiative to spend some time together to figure [the roles] out. We realized that this is a big machine here and it takes a lot of bandwidth to run it properly and to organize it properly, so we spent a fair amount of time scheming out ahead of time how all of this would be configured and how the responsibilities would be allocated." Ammann is now GM's president, and he is in charge of all of the company's international operations as well as its financial business.

Reuss, whom Ed Whitacre had favored to be CEO, says he didn't need to be part of those discussions. "I knew what I was going to do before they did," he says. "Nobody asked me if I wanted to do that, by the way," he says of the CEO role. Reuss is now executive vice president in charge of global product development, purchasing, and supply chain—the same job Barra previously held—and says he's enjoying the role and having Barra as his boss. "I'm really, really happy that it was her."

On December 9, 2013 the U.S. government sold the last of its shares in General Motors, whose stock had risen over the course of the year, in part because of the enthusiasm over new car models that had come out under Barra's watch. The next day, Dan Akerson announced his retirement, saying he needed to take care of his wife, who was ailing with advanced cancer.

His successor: Mary Barra.

At an employee town hall announcing the change, Barra said she was "honored" to be chosen. She also thanked Akerson for bringing "the spirit of winning" to the company. "Whether in quality, in great products or in financial results," Barra said, "If we're going to do it, we need to do it well." That spirit was a big change for GM, which in the prebankruptcy days had assumed that if it put products on the market, people would buy them. Barra had learned from Akerson that just being in the race wasn't enough.

Inside the company, Barra's elevation was met with a mixture of joy and relief. Joy at seeing the first woman CEO at a company in an industry heretofore run by white men. "You've got women thinking, 'Okay, this can be done; let me get engaged,'" says Sheena Bailey, who headed the company's women's network and works on the corporate governance staff. And relief because, after a bankruptcy and two CEOs from outside the company who showed little patience with the GM way of doing things, one of their own was back in charge.

Yes, Akerson and others called Barra a "change agent." But Barra was a known quantity who had grown up in GM. The warmth of her welcome was, in part, a measure of how hard she was going to have to work to convince everyone that it was no longer going to be business as usual at GM. From her time at the Fiero plant to working with Jack Smith to steering through the shoals of bankruptcy as an HR chief, Barra had had bosses who wanted to shake up GM's hidebound culture. None of them succeeded. And her buttoned-down, low-key manner made some question whether she was tough enough to do it.

Once she took over as CEO on January 15, Barra held her first senior leader meeting, gathering the top 300 or so global executives of GM into a packed Detroit ballroom. After giving a short presentation, she opened the floor up for questions, calling on most executives by name. "Being a lifer at GM, it was really great to see the CEO be able to answer all the questions, because she had worked in all the areas of business, and knew all the people by name," says Diana Tremblay, the fellow GMI graduate who was now running global business services. "It really felt good."

The feel-good moment was not going to last.

Notes

1. Ed Whitacre with Leslie Cauley, *American Turnaround: Reinventing AT&T and GM and the Way We Do Business in the USA* (New York: Business Plus/Hachette, 2013), 54.
2. "GM CEO Saw Barra as a Hidden Gem," *Automotive News*, October 24, 2011, 22.

3. Alex Taylor III, "Mary Barra: GM's Next CEO?" *Fortune*, December 24, 2012.
4. http://usnews.rankingsandreviews.com/cars-trucks/.
5. Alan Murray, "Women in a Man's World," *Wall Street Journal*, May 7, 2012, B11.
6. Tim Higgins, "CEO Akerson Led GM from IPO to End of Government Motors," *Bloomberg News*, December 11, 2013.

Chapter 12

Chevy Cobalt: End of the Honeymoon

Suddenly Mary Barra was no longer just an auto industry up-and-comer. She was a household name—the first woman to run a global automaker. She stared out from magazine covers and television screens. Her modest demeanor and Michigander accent, her working-class family, her childhood infatuation with cars, and most of all her rise from plant worker to plant manager to CEO were chronicled in virtually every U.S. media outlet, and a good portion of those abroad. Everything from her shoe selections to her pay package was scrutinized.

The latter got attention because her pay was far below that of Dan Akerson, even though the U.S. Treasury's strict rules about pay that she had negotiated with Kenneth Feinberg about following the bankruptcy were no longer in force since the government had sold its shares. Barra's annual salary for 2014 is $1.6 million, and her short-term incentive pay could reach $2.8 million on top of that for a total of $4.4 million. Akerson was paid a total of $9 million in 2013.

The pay gap got attention because women in top corporate positions still make on average 18 percent less than men do, according to Bloomberg data.[1] The five most highly paid executives in the Standard & Poor's 500 companies make $5.3 million on average, the data show— about 20 percent more than Barra. Barra told reporters that she respected the board's decisions, and later said that she had never asked for a raise during her whole career. Besides, the board was considering long-term compensation in the form of performance shares and restricted stock, which could increase her 2014 pay package to some $14 million.

While the size of her paycheck was making news, events were unfolding several tiers below Barra's level at General Motors that, when they finally burst into the open, would cast a shadow over her entire first year as CEO, and perhaps define her whole tenure.

On December 17, 2013, a week after Akerson announced he'd be handing over the reins to Barra, a group with the impenetrable name of the Executive Field Action Decision Committee (EFADC) met about some issues with the Chevrolet Cobalt. The compact car, which was in production from 2004 to 2010, had a troubled history of so-called moving stalls. Engineers at the company had known about it for some time, and several newspapers had even written about the problem as far back as 2005, when Barra was executive director of manufacturing engineering.

This December meeting of the committee was to discuss whether to recall the cars, which were stalling because of a faulty ignition switch.[2] This switch, which turns the car on and off, was susceptible to jostling: If it was tapped by a driver's knee or jolted when the car went over a bump, or the key chain was weighted down with multiple doodads, the switch could turn into the off position while the car was moving, even at highway speeds. The car's electrical systems would then lose power, meaning that its power steering and power brakes would be disabled. For years, this flaw had been classified as an inconvenience to drivers rather than as a potential safety problem, and at one point GM sent a service notice to its dealers about it. But incredibly, GM contended that it didn't appreciate that its engineers failed to connect the dots and understand that turning off the car's electrical system could also disable the air bags.

Though some car aficionados insist the vehicles could be steered off the road safely even without power, numerous accidents had resulted from the moving stalls. In cases where the air bags failed to deploy, the crashes could be fatal. At least 45 people have been killed as of this writing, and dozens more were injured. Adding to the tragedy, many of those who died were young, relatively inexperienced drivers in their first cars—the Cobalt as a compact was aimed at an entry-level market.

On that December day, though, only a handful of company officials were aware that any fatalities were involved. To recall the cars, all three members of the committee would have to agree. One committee member, head of engineering John Calabrese, asked numerous questions about the defect and the link between the switch and the air bags. The meeting was adjourned until January so that engineers could come up with responses to Calabrese's questions.

Calabrese, then a direct report of Barra's, informed her in late December that there was a problem with the Cobalt and that a recall was being considered, he told attorneys from law firm Jenner & Block, who were later hired by GM to investigate the matter.[3] He didn't mention that there were fatalities. Barra told him to "get the right data, then do the right thing."[4]

In the meantime, a day after the EFADC meeting, a lower-level contract worker at GM had ordered 500,000 new switches from parts supplier Delphi, according to e-mail traffic between the contractor and Delphi cited by the Wall Street Journal.[5] While that move seemed to indicate that the company was planning for a major recall, GM didn't alert either federal authorities at the National Highway Traffic Safety Administration (NHTSA) or its customers about the potentially fatal safety defect.

It was only on January 31, after a second meeting of the committee, that GM approved a recall of all the Chevrolet Cobalts and Pontiac G5s, which had the same switch, from model years 2005 to 2007. That would involve 780,000 cars. After getting the news from Mark Reuss, now head of global product development, Barra contacted Tim Solso, who had replaced Dan Akerson as the General Motors chairman, to let the board know.

"At first, none of us really understood the magnitude of the problem," says Solso, who was formerly the chairman of Cummins Engine. The recall was big, but not out of the ordinary for an automaker like GM, which sells close to 10 million cars a year.

Recalls generally are a fairly routine affair; automakers recall millions of cars annually. The reasons can vary dramatically, though: In some cases, a car may need to be inspected by a dealer for wear and tear of a specific part or a wire that could come loose; the problem might affect only a fraction of the recalled cars.

But recalls involving flaws that could kill people are not routine. By law, GM was required to let the NHTSA know about any safety-related recalls within five days. GM told the agency on February 7, and announced it to the public on February 13, with the added information that at least six deaths were attributable to crashes linked to the faulty switch.[6]

Barra's honeymoon was over. And things were about to get much worse.

Less than two weeks later, General Motors recalled an additional 800,000 cars—Chevrolets, Pontiacs, and Saturns—that had the same switch, bringing the total to 1.6 million vehicles. And the company raised the death toll that it attributed to accidents involving the switch to 13, and issued an apology for the deaths.

The NHTSA announced that it was investigating the company, and potentially would fine it the maximum $35 million. Two committees of Congress also began investigations, summoning Barra to appear before them. Meanwhile, attorneys began collecting claims for class action lawsuits, while the Justice Department began trying to determine whether there had been a criminal cover-up.

With the same frenzy that had followed her appointment only a couple of months earlier, columnists and commentators opined on how Barra would handle the challenge. Some even conjectured that Akerson had chosen her for the post and then beat a hasty exit because he knew the recall mess was about to break.[7] Akerson and Barra both vehemently denied that. The so-called "glass cliff" theory—that women only get to the top when the company is headed for a crisis—is "flawed," Barra said at a conference in December 2014.[8] "I doubt any company is that good," that it can see a crisis coming and promote someone in time to take the fall, she said.

Barra's response to the ignition switch recall took a page from the textbook of crisis management. She called reporters to GM's Detroit headquarters and repeated the apology the company had already made in official statements. "I want to start by saying again how sorry I am personally and how sorry General Motors is for what has happened," she said on March 18. "Clearly, lives have been lost and families are affected, and that is very serious. We want to just extend our deep condolences for everyone's losses."[9] She announced plans to name Jeff Boyer, a 40-year GM veteran who had studied at Barra's alma mater, General Motors Institute, as global head of safety. GM previously didn't have such a position.

The worst was yet to come, though. On March 29, the day before her first scheduled appearance before the transportation committee of the House of Representatives, GM dropped one more bomb: It was recalling *another* 980,000 cars from later model years that had been built with good switches, but might have received the faulty switch as a replacement part. The total of the recall was now 2.6 million cars—about a quarter of a whole year's output for the company.

It was then that Solso, who had joined the board only in June 2012, realized the company had "a huge problem." He adds that Barra has handled it with calm. "As a good leader, she's used the challenge as a catalyst for change," he says, adding that the board, which has the power to set her pay or fire her, continues to support her. Members of Congress would not be so understanding.

Before she testified, Barra met privately with the families of the victims of crashes to apologize and express her condolences. The small cars such as the Cobalt were inexpensive, and many of the victims were young people whose parents had bought them the cars. As some parents told her their stories, Barra shed tears.

She showed a steelier exterior facing the House panel. The hearing room looks like it was set up to intimidate witnesses. Members of Congress sit at a horseshoe-shaped, raised dais, glowering down at those being questioned. Barra sat at a long table in front of them. In the row behind her sat Michael Milliken, GM's chief counsel, Mark Reuss, and her friend Grace Leiblein, now the head of global purchasing and supply chain, which would buy parts such as the switch from suppliers. Directly behind them sat the families of people killed in the car accidents, many holding up large, framed photos of the victims.

In more than an hour of questioning, which was broadcast on live television, it emerged that not only had GM engineers known about the flaw in the ignition switch for years, but one of them had actually tried to fix it. He had the outside supplier revise the part so that it had more torque and wouldn't turn off the engine accidentally. He then failed to change the part number. The result was that the internal investigations into what went wrong with the cars kept coming up empty: When the switches were tested they all seemed to be fine. This essential nugget of information was in one of the thousands of pages of documents GM had sent to the committee.

How could that happen without anyone in the executive suite knowing about it? Why was the engineer in question still working at GM? Barra explained that the company had commissioned an investigation by Anton Valukas, an attorney whose firm, Chicago-based Jenner & Block, had worked for GM in the past. As the representatives pressed her for more detailed responses, she kept deferring to the Valukas investigation, which had only recently gotten under way.

Barra also told her questioners that she had hired Kenneth Feinberg, the former government special master of pay with whom she'd negotiated as head of human resources during GM's postbankruptcy months. Feinberg was charged with creating a compensation plan for victims of the switch.

But Barra declined to give any details of the program, or to say whether GM would compensate victims who bought cars before its bankruptcy, which shielded the new GM created in 2009 from lawsuits related to the old GM. Feinberg, who also oversaw compensation funds for victims of the 9/11 terrorist attacks and BP's 2010 oil spill, said Barra gave him independence in creating the fund and had provided no cap on the amount that he could pay potential victims. "It was the relationship we established when I was special master of pay that made her call on me," Feinberg says.

Some of the most tense interchanges came as Representative Paul Tonko of New York asked Barra whether she would commit to sharing the full contents of Valukas's report with the public. "We will share what's appropriate," she replied. "So you won't share the full report?" he pressed. "I commit that we will be transparent and share what's appropriate," Barra repeated.

The House testimony was just a warm-up for the main event the next day, though. Barra appeared before the Senate subcommittee on consumer protection, product safety, and insurance and for nearly two hours faced a barrage of questions from the senators, led by Claire McCaskill, a Missouri Democrat and former prosecutor. At both hearings, Barra sat impassively and in a performance that called to mind some of the Watergate hearings, repeating over and over again stock phrases that sounded like they had been written by the GM legal department: "That is part of the investigation" or "I don't have the complete facts to share with you today."

The senators grew increasingly frustrated with her nonanswers. This was a company that the U.S. government had bailed out just five years before with almost $50 billion of taxpayer money, they said, and here was the CEO stonewalling members of Congress, who represented taxpayers, about even the most basic details of the case.

One striking thing about the testimony had nothing to do with the recall itself. Here was a moment when the CEO of one of the country's largest companies was under withering attack from members of Congress, and not only was the person being questioned female, but so were most of the questioners. In fact, the harshest rebukes to Barra came from female senators. While only five of the committee's 13 members are women, four of them—McCaskill; Barbara Boxer, a California Democrat; Kelly Ayotte, a New Hampshire Republican; and Amy Kobluchar, a Minnesota Democrat—did the lion's share of the questioning. Neither side behaved in a stereotypically "female"—emotional or soft—way.

Still, Barra came across as more evasive than stoic. Asked repeatedly whether GM would take responsibility for the flaw, she replied, "We will make the best decision for our customers, recognizing that we have legal obligations and moral obligations." And she deflected many pointed questions, such as how it could be possible that GM engineers had known about the defect for years, yet done nothing. "That is part of the investigation," Barra said.

Boxer read out Barra's CV at GM since 2004, when the Cobalt problem first emerged, and asked her, after reading each job description, whether she wouldn't have known about the problems with the switch while working in that position. Barra replied in the negative each time. "So you know nothing about nothing!" Boxer said in exasperation. "I am very disappointed—really as a woman to woman—because the culture you're representing here today is the culture of the status quo."

Barra's stony performance, and her tense, tight-lipped expression during questioning, were replayed on news outlets around the world. The image was in stark contrast to just a few weeks before, when a smiling Barra had been mobbed at the Detroit Auto Show a day after taking on her new job.

The comedy writers at *Saturday Night Live* found it hard to resist. In a devastating follow-up to their 2008 roasting of Rick Wagoner's prebankruptcy testimony, the show that Saturday did a send-up of Barra in Washington. Comedian Kate McKinnon appeared as Barra in front of the congressional panel, and parroted her nonanswers such as "We are looking into that" to a variety of questions.

"When did *you* first learn about the ignition problem?" a "senator" asks.

"That's part of our investigation," McKinnon replies.

The befuddled-looking "senator" continues: "So you don't know when *you* knew?"

McKinnon replies: "I am looking into knowing when I first knew about it."[10]

Contrary to her poor public showing, Barra wasn't just waiting for the results of Valukas's report to take action. She made some changes, starting with her staff.

A few days after the *Saturday Night Live* skit, GM announced that the company's head of public relations and government affairs, Selim Bingol, had left the company, and that Barra was looking for a replacement.

Also departing was the head of human resources, Melissa Howell, who had been with GM since 1990. She was replaced by John J. Quattrone, a GM lifer who had previously worked for Barra as head of human resources for global product development, purchasing, and supply chain, and also while she ran HR. Quattrone had first met Barra in 1983, while she was still a co-op student working at the Fiero plant and he was working in HR for Pontiac. The human resources change came as Barra started implementing an internal program to empower employees to report safety issues without fear of retribution.

Both Bingol and Howell left "to pursue other interests."

To get the message across to employees, Barra set up an in-house program with an old GM style slogan: Speak Up for Safety. Staff of all levels were told they had to report to their managers any concerns they had about vehicle safety. If they didn't get a satisfactory response, they could contact Barra directly with their concerns.

Most significant, Barra ordered a deep dive into every pending safety recall at the company. And when there was any question of safety, the cars were recalled—and recalled. Over the spring and summer, it seemed as if a new GM recall was announced almost daily. By the end of the year, GM had recalled an incredible 32 million vehicles—more than the company sold in three years, and a record for a single automaker.

Barra says she was merely applying a lesson she learned, painfully, when the company had to be bailed out by the government. "What I learned from the bankruptcy is when you have a problem, you'd better solve it, because if you don't, generally six months from now it will be worse," she says. "Two or three years from now it may be gone—because you might be, too."

Barra also changed the recall process so that top executives would be involved in future decisions. Jeff Boyer, the head of safety, now reported to Mark Reuss. As CEO, Barra was not on the committee that approved recalls—the company had decided years earlier that top management should not have a say in whether cars were recalled, because they might have a conflict of interest. (CEOs were responsible for meeting the company's financial targets, and recalls cost money.) Now, she trusted Reuss to inform her quickly if any major recalls were needed. John Calabrese, the engineer who had been on the recall committee, retired at age 55.

"There are going to be more absolute recalls, but [involving] fewer ... cars," Reuss says, citing a recall in the summer of 2014 of just 20 Corvettes. Recalls can now happen in a couple of weeks, or even less, he says. "We'd like to not have recalls. But if we do have a recall we're going to get it sooner."

Amid the scramble to respond to the crisis, Barra made a point of communicating with customers and employees. She delivered updates on a special website for customers. And in early May, she kept a promise to speak to GM WOMEN, the employee women's group that grew from the one she created while working for Smith and Pearce in the 1990s.

"She was supposed to speak for 15 minutes and she stayed for an hour," says Charlie Gandy-Thompson, president of the group. "It was a pep talk. She told us, 'Just make sure you understand what you're doing;

focus on your job and not on what you see in the media.'" The message was especially welcome to Gandy-Thompson, who is an engineering manager in electrical validation and has been with the company for 20 years. Her team's job was to test and approve the replacement ignition switches. "It was very intense for me," she says. "Mary said, 'Make sure to focus; don't try to rush; make sure you get it right.'"

By late May, Valukas had finished his investigation of the recall. Jenner & Block lawyers had interviewed more than 230 witnesses and examined 41 million documents. The resulting 300-plus-page report was a powerful indictment of GM's corporate culture and its silos, where each department did its own work and failed to communicate with others, to the great detriment of its customers.

While the fault for approving and later changing the switch without changing its part number was laid at the feet of a single low-level engineer, Valukas and his staff concluded that the company shared the blame. It could have prevented many of the accidents if it had acted sooner, and that it had ignored many opportunities to do so.

"GM personnel's inability to address the ignition switch problem for over 11 years is a history of failures," the report said.[11] "Although everyone had responsibility to fix the problem, no one took responsibility."

Valukas cited what Barra described in her interview with his lawyers as "the GM nod," where everyone agreed in a meeting to a certain course of action, then went off and did nothing. GM had bungled multiple opportunities to look into and correct the defect: Customers, the media, and their own employees had warned of it at various times over the years, the report said.

Barra found the report a devastating indictment of the company. For decades, she had worked for CEOs who railed against GM's inward-looking culture and wanted to change it: Jack Smith, Ed Whitacre, and Dan Akerson. Now, here she was, CEO herself, confronted with an outsider's assessment that everything people had said about GM's culture—that it was bureaucratic and myopic, with no one taking responsibility—was true. She called the report "brutally tough and deeply troubling."

On June 2, Barra appeared at a town hall meeting that was beamed to GM employees worldwide. Marked by its emotion and controlled anger, Barra's speech was a defining moment for her leadership. She was contrite but also determined, not beaten down as she was in Congress. She was not going to let anyone off the hook. "For those of us who have dedicated our lives to this company, it is enormously painful to have our shortcomings laid out so vividly," she told employees, describing the devastating results of the Valukas investigation. She told them that she had fired 15 employees who either had not done their jobs regarding the flaw or had acted without any sense of urgency in investigating or responding to it. Those departing included the engineer who had approved the original faulty switch and then changed it without changing the part number, as well as several members of the legal department. The lawyers had negotiated settlements with some victims of the crashes but had not raised the issue with the head of the legal department or with other top executives.

"This report highlights a company that operated in silos," Barra said, "with a number of individuals seemingly looking for reasons not to act. This should never have happened." Then, as only someone who knew the culture could, she warned employees not to think that once the furor died down, things would go back to normal. She had already seen how executives' belief that it was "normal" for GM to get 50 percent of the country's auto sales had lulled the company into a complacency that helped lead it into bankruptcy.

"If we think that cleaning up this problem and making a few process changes will be enough, we are badly mistaken," she told the close to 1,000 workers who gathered to hear her speak live at the Warren technical center. "I *never* want to put this behind us. I want to keep this painful experience permanently in our collective memories. I don't want to forget what happened because I never want this to happen again."

Barra's speech was a departure from how such an event would have been handled in the past. Former GM chiefs would have closed ranks, or blamed a few bad apples and minimized the company's fault. "The old GM would have buried it," says former manufacturing executive Mark Sullivan.

Victims' families are not impressed, though, and have kept up pressure on the company and Barra to identify all those affected by the switch and to explain why it took so long to notify the public. With 45 deaths linked to the flaw as of early January 2015, safety advocates urged Feinberg to do more to find families of victims. The *New York Times* reported that a Yonkers, New York, woman named Brittany Alfarone was killed in a 2006 Chevrolet Cobalt in a single-car accident on October 9. The paper quoted her mother as saying she had twice tried to get the car fixed but was turned away by dealers.[12] "The Center for Auto Safety is concerned that the GM ignition compensation program will turn out to be little more than a public relations ploy for General Motors," Clarence Ditlow, the head of the center, wrote to Feinberg in November.

A few weeks after the Valukas report was released, Barra returned to Congress to provide the details that she had been unable to discuss in April. Though she still was treated sternly, the senators, in particular, gave her credit for her rapid response to the crisis. "I think you've handled this with courage and conviction and stepped forward," said McCaskill.

This time Barra, though still accepting blame for the crisis and expressing regret for it, no longer came across as a meek corporate automaton. She answered questions—when the senators didn't cut her off—and at times even fought back when she felt the senators were being unfair. McCaskill, for instance, said she couldn't understand "for the life of me" why Barra had not fired the company's chief counsel, Michael Milliken, for not knowing about the switch defect for so long. "This is either gross negligence or gross incompetence," McCaskill said, rolling her eyes.

"Senator McCaskill, I respectfully disagree," Barra replied, reiterating her promise to fix what is wrong with GM. "To do that, I need the right team. And Mike Milliken is a man of incredibly high integrity. He's got tremendous global experience as it relates to the legal profession. He's the person I need on this team."[13] Milliken, who also testified and apologized that day, sat in stony silence as the senators hammered home their point to Barra. Later in 2014, Milliken, aged 66, announced plans to retire in 2015.

Some of the senators were skeptical that someone who had spent her entire career at GM could change the culture that created "the GM nod," as described in the Valukas report. Here Barra seemed within a few inches of losing her cool.

"I've never accepted the GM nod and frankly I've called people out on it," Barra replied. When she spoke to the company's global staff in

June, she said, tapping her forefinger on the table for emphasis, "I told them that that behavior is unacceptable."

After this congressional appearance, no one made fun of her.

Notes

1. Carol Hymowitz and Cecile Daurat, "Best Paid Women in S&P 500 Settle for Less Remuneration," *Bloomberg News*, August 13, 2013.
2. Anton R. Valukas, "Report to Board of Directors of General Motors Company Regarding Ignition Switch Recalls," Jenner & Block, May 29, 2014. The chronology of the switch recall is based on pages 217–220 of the report.
3. Ibid., 220.
4. Ibid.
5. Jeff Bennett, "GM Ordered New Switches Long before Recall," *Wall Street Journal*, November 10, 2014.
6. Jeff Plungis and Tim Higgins, "GM's Cobalt Recall Follows Six Deaths on Switch Defect," *Bloomberg News*, February 13, 2014.
7. Joann Muller, "Why Do Women Think CEO Mary Barra Was Set Up to Take the Fall at GM?" *Forbes.com*, May 30, 2014.
8. "Managing Through Crisis," New York Times Dealbook conference, New York, December 11, 2014.
9. Jeff Green, "GM's Barra Says She's Personally 'Sorry' about Recall," *Bloomberg News*, March 18, 2014.
10. www.nbc.com/saturday-night-live/video/gm-hearings-cold-open/2770788.
11. www.nhtsa.gov/About+NHTSA/NHTSA+Electronic+Reading+Room+ (ERR).
12. Hilary Stout and Rebecca Ruiz, "Over One Million Cars Recalled by GM Still Await Defect Fix," *New York Times*, November 3, 2014, A1.
13. www.youtube.com/watch?v=IzrQz3Sl-_Q.

Chapter 13

Cadillac Escalade: Climbing Back

etroit's Eastern Market is in a gritty part of town where farmers sell stalks of brussels sprouts to urban families and to the bearded hipsters who are slowly bringing life to the formerly bankrupt city. Though only about a mile from General Motors Company's buttoned-down headquarters, it could be on a different planet. Colorful graffiti-covered warehouses alternate with rows of early 1900s brick buildings, where cafés and restaurants sprout like flowering weeds. The area takes its name from the largest open-air market in the country, created in 1891.

The symbolism of the place—history and renewal—isn't lost on Barra. She chose Eastern Market—instead of the chandeliered ballrooms of company confabulations past—as the locale for a meeting of her top 300 global executives in September 2014. The cream of GM gathered in a rehabbed warehouse on Russell Street, not far from the Hamtramck assembly plant that Barra once ran. The message she wanted to drive home was as unadorned as the surroundings: Either get with the program or get out.

Most of the meeting was spent discussing how managers behave, and how they need to change. Barra dislikes talking about corporate culture, because culture is an amorphous concept that develops over the course of many years—and can take that long to change. Previous CEOs of General Motors, dating back at least to Roger Smith in the 1980s, have promised that they would change the company's culture—with little noticeable effect.

"Behaviors," Barra says, "are something we can change right now, today." She adds that everybody at the company has to change his or her behavior, "including me." Her biggest fault: Being "too nice. I think I accepted a lack of performance if there was a reason. As managers, it's our job" to make sure people perform as they promised to. "You made your plan; now hit your plan."

She put that more demanding behavior into action even before the Russell Street meeting. She had asked each of the 300 leaders to send his or her thoughts about behaviors at the company that were holding it back. Most of them replied, but a couple dozen executives didn't. A year earlier, Barra might have accepted that someone was traveling internationally or having trouble with the survey software. But ignoring a request from the CEO is an example of the kind of behavior she is trying to change. The ones who failed to reply got a personal follow-up from Barra: I'm equating it with the fact that you don't care enough. And if you don't care enough, don't come to the meeting. If you do care enough, get it done and don't ever let this happen again.

Once the group was ensconced in Russell Street, Barra pulled no punches. At one point she called out the name of a manager from GM's manufacturing operations in Sao Jose dos Campos, Brazil, and asked him to stand. The manager, who had joined the company only a few months earlier, was unsure whether he was about to be made an example of. He was.

Barra read out his comment:

I'm new to GM, but it seems like the company doesn't understand that one person's problem needs to be everyone's problem, especially at this level.

The description almost exactly matched the company behavior criticized by Anton Valukas and others.

"That," Barra told him and the crowd, "is exactly what we need."[1]

It's a measure of how much that change is needed that even in this meeting, there was pushback. Some engineers argued that silos were necessary in technical areas because they needed the expertise to get things done. Then Johan de Nysschen, who previously headed Audi and whom Barra hired away from Nissan's Infiniti brand to be the president of Cadillac, disagreed, telling them there was a difference between silos, where one group works together but doesn't share information with others, and sharing technical expertise.

"If you think the system we have in place is the best one," Barra told the group, "you're part of the problem."

Her approach is the right one, says Maryann Keller, a longtime auto industry analyst who has written several books on GM. "The way you instill change is you have meetings and have people say what's wrong," Keller says. "You can't do it in a room full of people singing 'Kumbaya.'"

While top managers on Barra's team get her vision, making it trickle down to more than 200,000 employees will be more difficult. Talking about a vision for the future of the company will help galvanize employees who were demoralized by the ignition switch scandal, says Sigal Barsade, a professor of management at the University of Pennsylvania's Wharton School. "That's where her emotional intelligence comes into play," she says.

Barra harps on the idea that she will hold her employees accountable for how they do their jobs. That means up to and including firing for people who don't meet her standards, whether by lack of ability or by failing to follow orders. Though Barra says that she has been too forgiving, people who have worked with her over the years can recall instances where what her former mentor, manufacturing chief Gary Cowger, called the velvet glove came off and revealed the steel fist inside.

"I never observed her having any difficulty making people decisions, no matter how tough," says Ken Varisco, her boss in the 1990s, when Barra managed a group of a dozen or so people in manufacturing. He remembers Barra demoting another female executive who she felt wasn't up to the demands of the job. Barra herself talks about firing a couple of managers at the Hamtramck assembly plant who didn't agree with her game plan for how to overhaul quality. "They weren't really team players," Barra says.

She presided over waves of change while heading human resources in the months after the company's bankruptcy, helping Mark Reuss install many new sales and marketing executives, for instance. When Barra became head of global product development, she continued to remove people who didn't fit with her plans or who were in roles she felt were superfluous; she decided, for instance, to put one executive in charge of each car model, rather than three people as in the past.

Prior to the bankruptcy, General Motors would often try to find different positions for underperformers, says John Quattrone, who ran HR for Barra at product development and is now in charge of it globally. "Oftentimes it was a stretch," he says. "Mary realized you're not doing their careers any good and you're not helping the company."

Barra also didn't hesitate to fire those she held responsible for misbehavior, or failure to prevent misbehavior in their subordinates. In 2013, the Indian government began investigating a report that some GM staff had manipulated the environmental performance results for the engines on the company's Tavera model. GM recalled all 2005 to 2013 models of the Tavera, an SUV model sold only in India, "to address emissions and specifications issues." Barra, to whom the team that made the car reported, responded by ousting about a dozen staff who worked in the powertrain division, which develops and manufactures the engines.[2] Among those who departed were several long-serving managers, including a vice president who was a 44-year veteran of the company.

Following the Valukas report into the faulty ignition switch fiasco, Barra also made heads roll. Some 15 executives departed, including at least one at the vice president level and several top attorneys.

One of the best indicators of whether a CEO will be able to shake up a culture is whether he or she is willing to replace senior people, Barsade says. That's an especially hard task for an insider like Barra, who grew up with many of the top executives in the company. "She has to leverage her internal knowledge, and not let it stifle her as a change agent," Barsade says.

Barra has been doing that, but without as much fanfare as the post-Valukas firings. By December 2014—less than one year in her CEO job—Barra had swapped out top executives at a rapid pace as she assembled her management team. Of the top 18 officials at GM, 13 were either new to the company, in newly defined positions, or in expanded ones. Two of the remaining five had joined the company only a year earlier. One more, Michael Millikin, the general counsel who faced criticism over the ignition switch scandal, had announced plans to retire in 2015. And unlike the ranks of 50-and-older white men who've led GM in the past, Barra's team numbered several non-Americans, minorities, and women as well as executives in their 40s, including the president, Dan Ammann, a 42-year-old New Zealander. "Mary wants to get diversity of thought," says Quattrone, who is also one of the 13.

A New Team

In her first year on the job, Mary Barra reshuffled the responsibilities of some executives and replaced others, so that by December only **five** (names in boldface, below) of the 18 members of her executive team had been in their roles for more than a year. Two of those five had joined the company in 2013, and a third planned to retire in 2015, leaving just two members in the same roles they had under Dan Akerson.

1. DAN AMMANN, President
2. ALAN BATEY, President, North America
3. ALICIA BOLER-DAVIS, Senior Vice President, global customer experience and OnStar
4. TONY CERVONE, Senior Vice President, global communications
5. JIM DE LUCA, Executive Vice President, global manufacturing
6. ROBERT FERGUSON, Senior Vice President, global public policy
7. GERALD JOHNSON, Vice President, operational excellence

(Continued)

8. GRACE LEIBLEIN, Vice President, global quality

9. JOHAN DE NYSSCHEN, President, Cadillac

10. JOHN QUATTRONE, Vice President, global human resources

11. MARK REUSS, Vice President, global product development

12. CHUCK STEVENS, Executive Vice President, chief financial officer

13. MATTHEW TSIEN, Executive Vice President, president of GM China

14. JAIME ARDILA, Executive Vice President, president of GM South America

15. STEFAN JACOBY, Executive Vice President, consolidated international operations*

16. MIKE MILLIKIN, Executive Vice President, general counsel**

17. RANDALL MOTT, Senior Vice President, global information technology

18. KARL-THOMAS NEUMANN, Executive Vice President, president of GM Europe*

---

*Joined company in 2013.
**Plans to retire in 2015.
Source: General Motors.

In November 2014, Barra revamped the jobs held by the two women on her executive team, Alicia Boler-Davis and Grace Leiblein. Boler-Davis, a senior vice president, gave up oversight of quality, which she had been responsible for in addition to global customer relations. Boler-Davis, who led the company's response to consumers following the ignition switch affair, now focuses exclusively on customer relations and OnStar, which lets drivers connect to service representatives via their cars. Under Boler-Davis's watch, Barra and all the members of her management team take turns listening in on or responding to customer calls, to make them more aware of what is on consumers' minds—or, as Barra would put it, to make them more "customer-focused."

Grace Leiblein, Barra's friend and the former head of GM in both Brazil and Mexico, took over quality as a full-time role. She had most recently been in charge of dealing with the company's suppliers as vice president of global purchasing and supply chain management. With many of the 30,000 parts that make up cars today coming from outside suppliers, Leiblein's relationships could arguably help the company improve quality. "Quality is so important, it should be by itself," says Rosabeth Moss Kanter, a management professor at the Harvard Business School who has studied General Motors for decades. "Like pulling out safety, separating quality sends a signal that shows people at the company what is going to be valued."

One thing Barra doesn't value is the infamous "GM nod," which was skewered in the Valukas report and for which Barra was raked over the coals during her congressional testimony. Barra says she has called out people who looked like they were agreeing in a meeting and might then go back to their work and ignore any decisions made. Colleagues who've been in meetings with her say she asks people who don't speak during meetings about their point of view, to make sure she has their buy-in—or knows their objections—about any decisions that are being made. Now, when Barra ends a meeting with her staff, Quattrone says she admonishes them: "No meetings after the meeting."

Barra is also working on improving the way cars are built so that there will be fewer recalls in the future and certainly no more defects on the scale of the ignition switch disaster. In July 2014, the automaker began consulting with companies from the military, defense, and aerospace industries on production methods that would help lead to zero defects, or as close to that target as possible. Among those providing advice are the U.S. Navy's nuclear power department, Boeing Company, Virginia Tech, and Excelis, a maker of night vision software, whose board Reuss sits on. The aim, according to Reuss: "How do you design it defect free from day one, where there are no mistakes? You don't see nuclear power plants fail."

Simply hiring someone who did a stellar job at another company, rather than trying to find someone to promote from within, is a departure from the "old GM." De Nysschen, a South Africa native whom Barra hired in July, is one such outsider, who brought another radical— for GM—idea to the company. His first step as Cadillac president was to move the brand's headquarters to New York's Soho neighborhood from Detroit. Though only a few managers and sales and marketing staff are actually relocating, the change of locale sets a different tone for everyone. "New York is where luxury is defined," Barra told *Bloomberg News*. "It's much broader than the auto industry in terms of setting trends in luxury."[3]

Ammann was more blunt. "It is easy to sit in Michigan and conclude that Cadillac is performing well," he told the *Wall Street Journal*. "When you go to some of the coastal markets and see what's happening there, you realize that it is more of a challenge."[4] Whereas Cadillacs can frequently be seen on the highways around Detroit—Barra drives one herself—they are relatively rare on New York City's streets apart from some car-service companies.

De Nysschen says it could take a decade before the brand can make headway against luxury stalwarts such as Lexus, Mercedes, and BMW.[5] While sales of luxury vehicles increased about 8 percent in the United States in the first nine months of 2014, sales of Cadillacs declined 4 percent in the same period.[6] The drop came despite Cadillac's CTS model being named the *Motortrend* Car of the Year for 2014. Such awards will be for naught if consumers don't buy the cars. Barra has promised to introduce a new, larger Cadillac model in 2015 that will expand the brand's appeal to luxury consumers.

"Are they going to be fighting the Germans and Japanese, or have something different?" says Kevin Tynan, the auto industry analyst for Bloomberg Intelligence. He suggests focusing on Cadillac as an American luxury carmaker might be one way to distinguish the vehicles in the market.

Barra faces other challenges as well. The company still loses money in Europe, where Barra has promised GM will make a profit by 2016. Barra made the tough decision to stop selling Chevrolet cars there so GM can focus on its Opel brand, which has more name recognition among Europeans. In China, where the company now sells more cars than in any other country, competition is fierce and economic growth is slowing. In the United States, GM still relies heavily on sales of trucks for its profits; that's good when gas prices are low but leaves the company vulnerable if they rise and customers focus on smaller cars. Barra is betting that by introducing advanced communications and technology systems into cars, such as rear-seat entertainment, she'll be able to attract new customers to GM vehicles as well.

GM also needs to compete in a market that Barra says will undergo more change in the next decade or so than it has in the prior 50 years, thanks to technological advances. Consumers are increasingly looking for environmentally friendly vehicles, for instance, regardless of the price of oil. Traffic congestion is a growing concern, especially in emerging markets. Consumers in developing countries, where carmakers once sold stripped-down or outdated versions of their U.S. cars, now want the same kinds of features that consumers in developed markets seek. GM is moving into electric and hybrid vehicles such as the Chevrolet Volt, developed under Lutz and introduced while Barra was head of global product development, but its sales still lag behind those of Japanese-made rivals such as the Toyota Prius. And the car hasn't generated the same excitement as the TeslaRoadster, an all-electric sports car made by Tesla Motors.

The so-called connected car is one of Barra's focuses. She points to the auto industry's failure to capitalize on car phones when they were first introduced decades ago as a major missed opportunity. She's trying to make up for it now, installing 4GLTE into about 30 of General Motors' 2015 models. Customers "are clearly signaling that they want the connectivity they have in their smartphones integrated into their vehicles," Barra told a conference at Harvard in February 2014. The 4G vehicles are a step on the path toward autonomous cars, a technology GM is also developing.

"The connected car is even more important than the electric car," says Harvard's Rosabeth Moss Kanter, who is working on a book about the need to bring U.S. infrastructure up to modern standards. "The car will become an extension of all you have in your phone."

A connected car is a prerequisite for the developing technology of autonomous vehicles that Barra is also pursuing. For now, some vehicles are wired with sensors that can alert a driver if the car is straying from its lane, for instance, or brake when cars ahead slow down. Barra has promised that the 2017 model Cadillac CTS will be equipped with "vehicle-to-vehicle connectivity," allowing cars that have the technology to communicate with each other. The CTS will also have a system called Super Cruise that will allow hands-free driving for extended periods. Barra is working with Michigan officials and other automakers to install "smart" roadways on about 120 miles of highway around Detroit to test systems that will inform cars of obstacles or accidents ahead.

All the technological changes may work in Barra's favor when it comes to revamping the corporate culture, Kanter says. As cars increasingly rely on software rather than mechanical parts, the whole process of designing, making, and selling vehicles will be different. "It's a huge shift that's going to require an enormous change in the profile of employees," she says. "It will allow you to bring in people with a different profile and a different idea of what a car is."

The company can't be just a player in each of these areas; it needs to be a leader if it is to maintain profits and stem the decades-long slide in its market share, which stands at around 11 percent globally today, behind both Toyota and Volkswagen. And GM isn't only competing with traditional rivals; it also has to do battle with new entrants into transportation, such as Google and electric car maker Tesla. Not incidentally, both of the latter companies are based in Silicon Valley, where Barra studied at Stanford and whose spirit she'd like to instill at GM.

"I want it understood that the day of GM being a polite competitor is over," Barra said in a speech in Detroit in October, where, in front of a friendly hometown audience, she sounded more authoritative than she had in previous months. "We will be ethical, of course. But we will be tough, unrelenting competitors. … I have become impatient. I want to win. Not get by. Not hold on. Not be competitive. But win."[7]

What Barra needs to win most all, of course, is the faith of customers. Though other executives (at GM and outside), employees, and consultants say she has handled the ignition switch crisis well by confronting it head-on, apologizing publicly, commissioning an internal investigation, and hiring Kenneth Feinberg to compensate victims, the damage done to GM's image by the episode is immeasurable.

As of early January 2015, Feinberg had determined that at least 45 deaths were linked to the switch and eligible for compensation from the company, starting at $1 million. Dozens more claims were pending. In the meantime, GM as of late October had repaired only about half the recalled cars.

It seems likely that Barra will have to live with the specter of more legal action for the foreseeable future. Alleged victims were filing class action lawsuits against the company, which is trying to deflect legal actions that relate to cars purchased from the prebankruptcy GM. Car owners are also seeking compensation for the decline in the resale value of their vehicles. Meanwhile, the U.S. Justice Department is looking into whether there was a criminal cover-up. GM says it's cooperating with that investigation.

Barra, who says she's "all about hearts and minds," was working with another of her new hires—Tony Cervone, her former executive training classmate, who returned to GM in June to run global communications after stints at United Airlines and Volkswagen—to improve her image and that of the company.

In early September, she gave a talk about the future of automobiles at a global congress of the Intelligent Transportation Society, a group that aims to use technology to improve auto safety and mobility. There, Barra announced the plans to introduce cars that can communicate with each other, and thus avoid accidents, within two years. Later in September, she appeared on a panel at the Clinton Global Initiative in New York, a celebrity-studded affair that the former (and perhaps future) first family holds annually during the UN's annual General Assembly meeting. The panel on "valuing what matters" was moderated by Chelsea Clinton and dominated by Jack Ma, who was fresh off a record New York Stock Exchange listing for his Alibaba Group, which made the Internet entrepreneur China's richest man. His Alibaba Group raised $25 billion—25 percent more than the $20 billion that the new GM raised after exiting bankruptcy in 2010. There, Barra nodded energetically in agreement as Ma talked about his rise from humble roots, his focus on customers, and the potential of China's market.

Barra's presence at the Clinton event, and her appearance earlier in 2014 to hear President Obama give his State of the Union address, underlined something that can be overlooked in the day-to-day business of running a company, especially one like GM that has been under siege. She is a barrier-breaking woman, and her mere existence at the top of General Motors can help galvanize future generations of young women to follow in her footsteps.

The evening of the Clinton meeting, Barra accepted an award for social responsibility from the Appeal of Conscience Foundation, a little-known New York group that annually honors heads of state and companies. There, Barra paid tribute to GM's efforts at diversity, adding that she was a beneficiary of those policies. In October, she was feted in Los Angeles as one of *Fortune* magazine's most powerful women. Later in the month, she was hailed as a "hometown hero" by the Detroit Economic Club and given a manufacturing award by the University of Michigan, where she had been the commencement speaker in May. She also appeared on the covers of *Time* and *Forbes* magazines.

The swirl of honors was cut short in mid-November, just days before Washington's National Women's History Museum was slated to present her with the Katherine Graham Living Legend Award, named after the late Washington Post Company leader, the first woman to become a Fortune 500 CEO. The family of one of the ignition switch victims and a Washington-based organization called the National Legal & Policy Center wrote to Congress and the museum objecting to Barra receiving the award. "We believe that Barra should focus on GM's remaining safety problems before traveling around the country to accept awards," wrote Peter Flaherty, the organization's president. A day later, GM announced that Barra would not go to Washington to accept the award.

Though the Valukas report into the ignition switch fiasco said Barra had no knowledge of the defect until December 2013, she is still facing lingering anger from victims and other members of the public for the company's failure to disclose it sooner. Those sentiments, and the pending legal actions, aren't likely to disappear any time soon. And for all Barra's focus on teamwork, the decisions about what direction to take going forward are ultimately hers as CEO. Things will happen that no one can predict: a recall crisis, a war, a trade barrier, an oil price swing, or tough new legislation. She'll have to react. Though she didn't create the problems GM has today, they are now hers. She's responsible for fixing them and for steering the company onto a path toward success instead of perpetual decline.

It's an enormous job. But if anyone is up to the task, Barra is. Though she says she never dreamed that one day she would be the CEO of General Motors, she has spent her whole career preparing for this role. From straight-A student to plant manager, from human resources boss to overseer of product development, her intelligence, humility, and loyalty to the company have earned her a legion of fans who are rooting for her.

Barra deserves to be celebrated for breaking the glass ceiling and reaching the pinnacle of an industry that has been dominated by men. But she can't afford to pause and enjoy the view. She has matched the achievement of generations of organization men just by being where she is today. Now she has to surpass them, by ensuring the future of one of America's most storied companies. Her job is only beginning. History, and Barra's employees, customers, and shareholders, will hold her accountable for the results.

Notes

1. The meeting in Detroit was described by Tony Cervone.
2. Tim Higgins and Rajesh Kumar Singh, "GM Fires Several Employees after India SUV Recall," *Bloomberg News*, July 26, 2013.
3. David Welch and Madeleine O'Leary, "GM Makes Cadillac a Separate Unit, Plans Office in NYC," *Bloomberg News*, September 23, 2014.
4. Jeff Bennett, "GM's Ammann Drives for Change," *Wall Street Journal*, November 11, 2014.
5. Aaron M. Kessler, "Cadillac Tries to Make a Fresh Start in New York," *New York Times*, September 24, 2014, B1.
6. Bloomberg Intelligence data, October 1, 2014.
7. Speech to Detroit Economic Club, October 28, 2014.

Chapter 14

Buick Encore: Finding the Next Mary Barra

When Mary Barra started her career in the early 1980s, women were making inroads in the workplace. A series of laws enshrining civil rights and equal pay had put corporate decision makers on notice that they could no longer ignore women and minorities when it came to hiring and promotions.

Popular culture, starting in the 1970s when Barra was growing up, had made the so-called liberated woman into a new stereotype, repeated in commercials, films, and television shows. "The 1970s were a real tipping point: There were more women in the labor force than out of it, and the birthrate dropped below the replacement rate for the first time," says Kathleen Gerson, a sociology professor at New York University who studies gender. "There was a mass change of consciousness, and it became increasingly obvious that the doors were starting to open for women."

Women were still something of a novelty in the workplace. Those who wanted to get ahead aimed to blend in and call as little attention to their gender as possible. They even dressed a bit like men, favoring business suits accessorized with floppy bow ties (for an example, check out Barra's college yearbook photo in the insert).

At about the same time, an important shift took place in the U.S. educational system. Women began to outnumber men when it came to earning college degrees. That change happened starting with women born in 1956[1]—five years before Barra. Today, women outnumber men in earning undergraduate degrees by a three-to-two margin and also earn more graduate degrees. Women now make up 48 percent of the labor force in the United States—not parity exactly, but pretty close.

However, when you look at the so-called STEM fields—science, technology, engineering, and mathematics—we could be right back in the 1970s again.

Though about 30 percent of Barra's graduating class of 1985 at General Motors Institute (now Kettering University) was female, the women were concentrated more in the less technical management majors. Barra's electrical engineering section, considered harder than other majors because of all the math involved, had 17 women out of 64 graduates—about 26 percent.

Kettering still has cooperative work-study programs, but is no longer owned by General Motors. So students can choose engineering internships at dozens of companies, including GM and other auto industry suppliers located in the area. Today, fewer than 20 percent of the school's students are women.

Kettering isn't unusual when it comes to women engineers. That percentage is in line with, or better than, the average at university engineering programs worldwide. Nationwide, only 15.8 percent of college graduates in science and engineering are women.[2]

Why are the numbers so low?

It's not a lack of ability. An analysis published in the American Psychological Association's *Psychological Bulletin* in 2014 found that girls have an edge over boys in school marks in all subjects, including math and science, contradicting popular stereotypes. The authors analyzed hundreds of previously published scientific studies to arrive at their con-clusion, adding, "The fact that females generally perform better than their male counterparts ... seems to be a well-kept secret considering how little attention it has received."[3]

The Girl Scouts of the USA set out to understand the gap in a survey of teen girls' attitudes toward STEM subjects and careers. The study, which polled a national sample of 852 teens, found that 74 percent of them were interested in STEM subjects.[4] Among the girls who said they were interested in STEM subjects, though, the proportion who said they would be interested in STEM-related careers, especially engineering and computer science, was far lower. Only 32 percent were interested in pursuing engineering, and just 27 percent were interested in information technology.

The Girl Scouts study made several recommendations about main-taining girls' interests in STEM subjects as they consider what they'd like to study in college. Because of their good grades in all subjects, girls have options beyond STEM fields. They need to understand that they could accomplish their life goals, such as helping people, working in teams, and solving problems, in STEM careers as well as in other areas such as teaching or non-profits. And they need to be exposed to people who are working in these careers, especially women. "Girls can recognize how women in these fields have succeeded and overcome obstacles," the report says.

Cathy Clegg has been GM's vice president in charge of North Amer-ican manufacturing—a job Barra formerly held—since June 2014. She remembers well how her middle school guidance counselor tried to pigeonhole her into stereotypical female roles. "I've always liked sci-ence and math," she says. "In ninth grade I took this aptitude test, which had different categories. My scores were something like spatial relations, 98; analytical, 97; natural science, 98; ... clerical speed and accuracy, 17. I can remember sitting down with my counselor, and she was just upside down: 'What are you going to do? What are you going to *do*?'" The counselor could see only that Clegg was poor at clerical speed and accuracy, skills needed for a secretarial job, not that she was gifted in math and science. Clegg says she was helped by the fact that her par-ents supported her choice of career—especially her father, who was a

manufacturing executive at GM. Today Clegg manages 74,000 people
at 55 plants in North America.

Barra believes that girls, particularly those around middle school age,
need to be better informed about how STEM subjects relate to different
careers—even those that aren't typically thought of as science or math
related. Her own high school age daughter is interested in fashion; for
that you need to know about materials and geometry and how things are
made. "It all starts with a love of math and science, and really cultivating
that in the sixth, seventh, and eighth grades," Barra says.

She visited a school in Detroit and asked children what they wanted
to be when they grew up, and found she could make science or math relevant to virtually every career. "I think people really don't know what
an engineer does," she says. "We don't do a good-enough job relat-
ing math and science to real life so that they don't want to step away
from it."

That would help to get more girls into the pipeline. But there are
still problems keeping them there. A survey of more than 5,000 women
conducted by academics at the University of Wisconsin–Milwaukee[5]
and supported by the National Science Foundation found that while
about 20 percent of engineering graduates are women, they make up
only 11 percent of those working in engineering.

Many women left the field because they didn't like the workplace
climate or they felt there wasn't enough opportunity for advancement.
A total of 10 percent never even entered the field after earning
their degrees, the researchers said, because they thought there wasn't
sufficient support for women and they believed the field was inflexible.
In fact, the percentage of women who never enter engineering
despite having a degree has increased to about 23 percent in the
past decade, from just over 5 percent in the early 1980s, when Barra
studied.

Women have misconceptions about what it's like to work as an engineer, says Nita Patel, the international chairman of the global Women
in Engineering section of the Institute of Electrical and Electronics
Engineers (IEEE), who wasn't involved in the research. "Actually, engineering is one of the most flexible professions when it comes to letting
you work at home, because it's project driven," she says.

Patel adds that women who take time off to have children may have trouble getting back into the field unless they keep abreast of developments by taking classes or reading industry journals. "Even if you're out of the industry for three or four months, the skills change really rapidly," she says.

Still, a quarter of women who enter the engineering field leave by the time they are 30, according to the Society of Women Engineers. Many of them wind up working in other fields instead. Catalyst, the New York–based group that advocates for women in business, did a study in 2014 that lays the blame in part on women feeling like outsiders at tech companies, without a sufficient number of sponsors—female or male—to help them navigate their careers. In these companies, even women who were working in non-STEM roles, such as finance or management, felt left out. The study found "a pervasive cultural problem in STEM industry companies that makes it particularly challenging for women at all ranks—whether they're working in tech roles or on the business side."[6]

As CEO of GM, Barra is a model of what young women interested in science and math can achieve, but she's not an outlier. There are other women in STEM fields who have risen to the top as well: Ursula Burns, a mechanical engineer who is CEO of Xerox and who is even more unusual at the top as an African American woman; Ginny Rometti, who studied both computer science and electrical engineering, is IBM's first woman CEO; and Yahoo!'s Marissa Mayer is a computer science graduate. Women are also CEOs of two defense technology companies: Lockheed Martin, led by Marillyn Hewson, an industrial engineer, and General Dynamics, whose chief Phebe Novakovic is a former CIA agent. Barra is a member of the General Dynamics board.

Barra wears the mantle of feminist role model uneasily. She takes pains to say that she had a long string of male mentors who helped her. And she shows little patience for women who complain that they're treated unfairly because of their gender. She recalls a meeting of Inforum, the Michigan women in business organization that she attended while former University of Michigan president Mary Sue Coleman was speaking. "A young woman in the audience said, 'What should I do if I'm not being given the same opportunities and not being paid as much?' and she said, 'Work harder!' I've always thought that was a brilliant answer," Barra says. "No matter where you are, everything's not perfect; life's not fair, so get over it. And you don't have to be a woman to have that happen to you."

Mary Barra's Career Advice

1. Do what you're passionate about. You'll do it for a long time, and if you're passionate about it you'll have better results.
2. Do the work. Even if you're not happy with your current job, do it well. If you're working harder than everyone else, you'll get opportunities. Control what you can control, and put that energy in.
3. Own your own work/life balance. Figure out a way to blend your personal life and your professional life and make those trade-offs. Then, understand what those trade-offs are.
4. Be honest. You'll be tested at some point, so do the right thing even if it's hard. You can never go back if you don't.
5. Own your own career. Research what's needed to do the job you want to do—talk to the people who have that job to find out what it's like. Let your boss know what you are aspiring to be so he or she can give you opportunities when they arise.

Barra's advice for younger women who would like to follow in her footsteps is: "Do the work. Don't worry about what you can't control; control what you can, and put that energy in."

She certainly has done that in her own career, and was never known to be someone who complained about her lot—even when she was doing a job she didn't particularly want. She claims to have never once asked for a raise during her career; she thought that doing the work would be enough, and things would even out in the end. "If you're working harder than everyone else, it's not going to matter what your gender is," Barra says.

Of course, Barra works at a company that has a highly articulated system for finding and advancing talented women. Even before

General Motors settled a discrimination lawsuit with the Equal Employment Opportunity Commission in 1983, company executives had decided that it made sense to hire and promote women. Barra was part of a cohort of several dozen women who were trained and given opportunities for advancement, beginning in the late 1970s and early 1980s and continuing throughout her career.

"GM had a very active development program for women," says Annette Clayton, who was one of those women. She worked at GM for 23 years before being headhunted away by Dell Computer, and now works for Schneider Electric in supply chain management. "You could tell we were being targeted for key experiences and accelerated through them." Clayton sat on the company's North American strategy board in the early 2000s, while Rick Wagoner was CEO. She and two other women were present while major corporate decisions were made. Clayton later went on to lead the company's Saturn car unit. Others being fast-tracked were Grace Leiblein, Barra's friend and the former head of GM Brazil and Mexico, and Diana Tremblay, who spent time in Europe as well as at different U.S. locations of GM.

Today, those women are in their 50s and many of them have made it into the top executive echelons. Some, like Clayton, have left the company but hold senior positions elsewhere.

To look at GM's leadership is to see a strong representation for women, in addition to Barra: GM has four women on its 12-member board of directors, or 33 percent (there were five, but one retired in 2014).

When a Detroit high school student asks Barra how she got to be the head of a company in a male-dominated industry, she first answers, "I don't agree that it's a male-dominated industry," before going on to talk about needing to work hard and the help she has gotten from mentors.

She is wrong about the auto industry, though, and about GM. Both are overwhelmingly dominated by men. GM's total global workforce of 219,000 people is only 17.6 percent female. The number rises to 23 percent when only the 74,000 salaried workers, not the hourly plant laborers, are counted, according to company figures.

Those percentages are far worse than the ones reported by Silicon Valley tech companies such as Apple, Facebook, Google, and Twitter,

Afterword

In researching this book, one thing became clear: the important role played by external support, both personal and institutional, in helping women like Mary Barra succeed. That may sound obvious, but for a huge number of companies and professions, it's not.

Support is not simply the matter of having an assigned mentor, or a women's group, though those things can certainly help. It's an organic process, starting with a family environment where girls are encouraged in their interest in science, technology, engineering, and mathematics (STEM) subjects and their abilities are nurtured. Teachers and guidance counselors also need to be on the lookout to encourage girls to follow their interests. Universities need to seek out female students for those fields, rather than waiting for them to apply. Throughout their schooling, girls need to be treated with equal respect in the classroom. Barra is consistently cited as "an excellent listener"—by men. Listening is important, but it helps to put those comments in context to read what Princeton University's Anne-Marie Slaughter writes in her 2012 essay about what's holding women back in their careers:

> I continually push the women in my classes to speak more. They must gain the confidence to value their own insights and questions, and to

present them readily. My husband agrees, but he actually tries to get the young men in his classes to act more like the women—to speak less and listen more.[1]

Our Barra wannabe, should she graduate with her STEM degree, next needs to land with an employer that recruits, trains, and provides a career path for talented women. Say what you will about GM's corporate culture—that same bureaucratic and inward-looking culture that is so often criticized—but it has had systems and processes in place for decades to make sure that the company has hired, trained, and promoted women. Managers have been judged, in part, by their records at hiring and advancing women and minorities. There were and still are metrics related to diversity that all managers are held accountable for. The systems took time to develop, and required a jolt in the form of a lawsuit from the Equal Employment Opportunity Commission (EEOC) in the 1970s (settled a decade later) to help get started in earnest. But the systems were in place.

Of course, no matter how many systems you have to promote women, you need to find people who are talented. Barra is smart and has great people skills—virtually everyone I talked to agreed. But she was able to make her talents known and to develop them, thanks in very large part to the corporate structure that encouraged managers to look for people like her, and when they found them, to develop them. Barra didn't get any special treatment for being female. She simply was admitted into the club that for decades had been reserved for talented men. She got the same kind of mentoring, promotions, and training that the men did. Had she *not* had that help, she might still very well be toiling away as a respected midlevel manager in manufacturing, rather than leading the company.

All of the preceding is not to be "nice," as Barra says, but because it's good business practice. "Don't you think customers pay attention when they see the senior management team of GM and it's all white and all male?" asked Harry Pearce, the former vice chairman who helped set up those systems. "You're denying yourself these incredibly rich resources. Why don't we unleash the power of *all* the people out there?"

Though many countries—such as Norway and France—have instituted quotas for women on corporate boards, there is virtually no chance that system could be adopted in the United States. And as far as I know, no company has quotas for female managers. So what should companies that want to advance women do? They should ask, "Where are the women?" If a job is open and no women are interviewed, why not? If a department is all male, the manager needs to be asked why. Often, these choices aren't made to intentionally exclude women, but executives need to be made aware that they should be seeking out the most diverse range of candidates for any position. Corporations can help them find qualified female candidates, internally or externally. If the best candidate is male, fine; there is no obligation to hire a woman. But there should be an obligation to seek them out.

Once a woman is hired and she shows herself to be capable, her employer needs to support her. She may want to join resource groups, get one-on-one coaching, and have flexible working hours. Managers should recognize that men want some of those things, too, especially the younger generation.

It took GM more than 100 years to produce a Mary Barra. Younger companies can learn from Barra's experience and build some of the pathways to power into their own systems. They have to. Companies can't afford to shut out half the population—and half their potential customers.

Note

1. Anne-Marie Slaughter, "Why Women Still Can't Have It All," *Atlantic,* July/August 2012.

Appendix

Barra Biography

As a "high-potential" employee, Barra was cycled through different roles at General Motors every couple of years—and sometimes more often. The company also paid for her MBA studies at the Stanford Graduate School of Business.

1961: Born December 24, Waterford, Michigan.

1980: Graduates from Waterford Mott High School, Waterford, Michigan. Voted most likely to succeed.

1985: Bachelor of Science in Electrical Engineering, General Motors Institute (GMI; now Kettering University), Flint, Michigan. Works as a co-op student at Pontiac Motor division.

1985: Marries Tony Barra, another engineering graduate of GMI.

1985–1988: Senior plant engineer and general supervisor, Pontiac Fiero plant, Pontiac, Michigan.

1988–1990: Master of Business Administration, Stanford University, Stanford, California, as a General Motors Fellow.

Taylor, Alex, III. *Sixty to Zero: An Inside Look at the Collapse of General Motors—and the Detroit Auto Industry*. New Haven, CT: Yale University Press, 2010.

von Neumann Whitman, Marina. *The Martian's Daughter: A Memoir*. Ann Arbor: University of Michigan Press, 2013.

Whitacre, Ed, with Leslie Cauley. *American Turnaround: Reinventing AT&T and GM and the Way We Do Business in the USA*. New York: Business Plus/Hachette, 2013.

About the Author

LAURA **C**OLBY is a reporter at large at Bloomberg News in New York, writing about women in the global economy and education. She was previously Managing Editor of *Bloomberg Markets*, an award-winning monthly magazine that provides in-depth coverage of global finance and business. She has also been London bureau chief at Institutional Investor, international editor of *Fortune* magazine and a reporter and editor based in Paris, Rome, and Brussels for the *Wall Street Journal* and the *International Herald Tribune*.

Colby, who grew up in a New York City suburb where her family always had a GM car parked in the driveway, now lives in Brooklyn.

Index